In
DEFENCE *of* DOUBT

AN INVITATION TO ADVENTURE

SECOND EDITION

VAL WEBB

Val Webb

WIPF & STOCK · Eugene, Oregon

Wipf and Stock Publishers
199 W 8th Ave, Suite 3
Eugene, OR 97401

In Defence of Doubt, Second Edition
An Invitation to Adventure
By Webb, Val
Copyright©2012 Mosaic Press
ISBN 13: 978-1-62564-314-8
Publication date 7/29/2013
Previously published by Mosaic Press, 2012

LIST OF OTHER BOOKS BY VAL WEBB

John's Message: Good news for the new millennium (Abingdon Press, 1999)

Why We're Equal: Introducing feminist theology (St. Louis, MO: Chalice Press, 1999)

Florence Nightingale: The making of a radical theologian (St. Louis, MO: Chalice Press, 2002)

Like Catching Water in a Net: Human attempts to describe the Divine (New York & London: Continuum, 2007)

Stepping out with the Sacred: Human attempts to engage the Divine (New York & London: Continuum, 2010)

Contents

Preface to the Second Edition

The publication of a book is the birthing of an idea or the lived experiences of its author. Like water under pressure, the plot begins either as a small trickle that climaxes in an orderly flowing river, or it breaks out with all its passion into a raging torrent. Once released, like a river flowing through new territory, a book takes on a life of its own, independent of the author. Its ideas evolve, from the initial shape of the author's need to speak, into the shape of the reader who drinks the words, experiences and ideas, ingesting and adapting them into her own context and experience.

In Defence of Doubt began writing itself within me many, many years ago, not as formed words but as thoughts and reflections on my experiences with doubt and how this totally affected who I was. Many events along the way are responsible for this internal voice being "heard to speak", some of which I mention in this book. But what finally makes a person write down such thoughts in the shape of a book, not just for herself, but hesitantly offering her inner being to the world? Sometimes it is simply a space of time in which to work, a change in circumstance.

For me, such a summer happened when I moved to the United States from Australia in 1988 for a second extended stay. It seemed the moment to write, even though the story is still far from ended. A number of publishers who received my manuscript for consideration did not agree until, instead of the usual three-paragraph rejection letter, the telephone rang. I can remember vividly which room I was in, whether I was standing or sitting and most of that conversation with Dr. David Polk, editor of Chalice Press. Perhaps only another writer will understand the magic of such a moment.

From phone call to contract to published product took four years, during which time both of us wondered what would be the outcome. The book became a reality in 1995, no longer just something I had written of my journey with doubt, but now an invitation for the reader's own adventure. Whether you resonate with what has been written depends on the particular convergence of experiences that constitute you at the moment of reading. My hope, and the reason I wrote *In Defence of Doubt,* is that it might nudge many readers to face their particular moments of existence with honesty, courageous doubt and an openness to adventure. Life is all too short to be lived in a shape provided by others. As Florence Nightingale said towards the end of her amazing life, "Live your life while you have it. Life is a splendid gift. There is nothing small in it". [1]

It is now seventeen years since this book was first published. During that time, I have received countless letters from people thanking me for bringing their hidden thoughts into the light and allowing them to embrace doubt as a constructive aid for life. As one church leader wrote, "Every congregation ought to secure several copies of this book and circulate them among the membership — but only if those 'in authority' are willing to allow members to doubt, question, and challenge the status quo of beliefs found in most churches". [2] Another used the book in a church study group and wrote "When doubt is reclaimed as a gift, then deeper levels of community and faith may be experienced by those committed to seeking together". [3] However, the bulk of letters received, and those that continue to reach my inbox, come from ordinary people who sit in pews and have never before been affirmed in their doubts but made instead to feel somehow responsible and to blame. Such feedback has made the whole process of writing more than worthwhile.

In this second edition, the bulk of the book has not changed except to update some historic events, add a few recent doubters to the pool, include a chapter on progressive Christianity and new theological directions and broaden the last chapter on world religions. I will always treasure the reaction of my father (who has since died) to this book. Having grown up in a religious climate where doubts were not encouraged, I wondered what he would think of my "heresies". He was an academic in agriculture and had worked in developing countries all over the world with people of many different faiths. He was also a prominent figure in mission societies and a lay preacher. He placed the book on the table before me when he had finished it and said, "Wonderful! I especially liked the last chapter on truth in other religions. That's what I've always really thought as well!"

A preface serves to thank those who contributed to the book, yet how can anyone thank all the people who networked and converged, often unconsciously, to bring an author and book to pass? For all of them, thank you that your lives somehow interconnected with mine and opened new doors for me. In the first edition, I acknowledged the following:

- My parents, Joan and Perce Skerman who raised me with the irrefutable assumption that faith is the *raison d'être* for living. While I may have embraced some theological ideas different from theirs over the years, they have loved me in all my different modes

- The hundreds of writers whose books have formed bridges for me from one doubt to another and kept the process alive in me. In gratitude, I humbly hope that this book may be a bridge for others

- David Polk of Chalice Press, an editor who believed in me and the manuscript in an act of faith probably mixed with a sprinkling of healthy doubt as well.

- My colleagues at university and seminary who mentored me and the others who despaired of my theology. Some of the best adventures are born out of a determination to be honest with oneself despite the prevailing culture and consequences

- My children Helen, Paul and Karen, wonderful adults whose lives fill me with such joy and who share their adventures of discovery with me. To be a mother has been my greatest adventure of all, the most enduring reminder of the interconnectedness and mutuality of life. I hope the risk I have taken in exploring doubts rather than certainties openly with them has been freeing for them as well

- My husband Maurice Webb, where anything I say about the adventure of life lived with him would be an understatement. Thank you for keeping me company on the way and being my best friend.

In this second edition, I add my ongoing thanks to Chalice Press who marketed my first edition and to all those who warmly embraced it and encouraged me to continue writing. Such enthusiasm assures an author that there is more to say — and more boldly, hence my ninth book being published in 2010. I would like to thank Hugh McGinlay and Mosaic Resources whose gentle affirmation as Australian distributors for my books has led to the publication of this second edition by their own Mosaic Press. I also acknowledge with much love my extended family since the first edition - my children's spouses Steve, Alexis and Sean, and my incredible grandchildren, Dan, Rhys, Kyle, Calvin, Max, Lola and Jake. At such momentous times of birthing something new that goes on to interact with others independent of you, the world stops for just a second in anticipation and we realize again in that instant that no one acts or thinks or loves alone. Val Webb

---

[1] Florence Nightingale, quoted in Val Webb, *Florence Nightingale: the making of a radical theologian* (St. Louis, Mo: Chalice Press, 2002), 21

[2] William McDermet III, *The Disciple,* July/August 1995, 32

[3] Nancy Victorin Vangerud, *Daughters of Sarah,* Fall 1995, 71

Chapter 1.   *Introduction to Doubt*

The first key to wisdom
is assiduous and frequent questioning ...
for by doubting we come to inquiry,
and by inquiry we arrive at truth.

Peter Abelard (1079-1142) [4]

"He's naked!" the little boy shouts to his mother. A hush captures the cheering crowd as horrified eyes search for the culprit. Then the ripple starts, swelling to an explosion of laughter and relief. The emperor *is* naked. The talk about the new court fashions is a charade. Yet no one in the subservient crowd was brave enough to call it so, until the emperor in all his silliness paraded before a little boy. Fools may tread where angels fear to roam, but the little boy was no fool. He was young and honest enough not to have been silenced by societal pressure. The little boy doubted what everyone else doubted but would not admit, even though the facts - and the emperor - lay bare and exposed.

Doubt is the theme of this book - honest, creative, courageous doubt; doubt that moves us from a confining space to a place of freedom; doubt that is recognized as the active agent in all of life - science, politics, education and more. Doubt is not ignorance or lack of faith or understanding. It is the nagging question that still remains despite great attempts to solve or deny the problem.

Such healthy doubt is the root of new knowledge. If learning is simply the sponge-like absorption of answers, learning is indoctrination. Valid acquisition of knowledge challenges us to question answers, theories and even the questions. Without such creative doubt, the earth would still be flat, diseases the curses of evil spirits and travel to the moon impossible. Human progress has depended on courageous people who doubted the status quo, refused to be silenced by the nodding crowd and believed in the possibility of new ways of thinking.

Doubt is encouraged in most disciplines of learning today, yet somehow when doubt rears its head in religious conversation, there are many who insist we abandon all creative questioning and give blind acquiescence like the emperor's loyal subjects. Since the day poor Thomas was labelled for refusing to believe without seeing the physical evidence, doubt has strangely scored a negative vote in religion. Theologian Frank Rees (1950-) says:

> The existence and nature of God, the transcendent uncreated ground and source of all life, is for us the ultimate mystery. In response, a strong measure of doubt would seem appropriate as a recognition of our unknowing. Yet, throughout Christian history, doubt has been seen as inappropriate. Teachers and pastors have enjoined their people not to doubt, while theologians have sought to explain how faith is to be understood in a way that overcomes doubt. [5]

Like the fat, naked ruler, doctrines are still paraded by us today with trappings from earlier eras that scarcely cover their "nakedness". Where are the doubters, the little boys and girls who cry out, verbalizing the nagging inconsistencies that tug at the minds of the rest of us waving dutifully beside the road?

This book is not for those who say they never doubt. They may be content in their uncomplicated world. It is for those whose life has been, and still is, a constant dialogue with doubts about what they hear as Christian beliefs. It is for those who warm church pews but live a dualistic existence, switching off to discrepancies in the stories but not wanting to give up the camaraderie of the faithful. It is for those whose doubts have forced them out of the religion of their youth because those dogmas no longer make sense to them. It is for those who turned to religion as adults but found its teachings irrelevant, inflexible, and alien to experience.

This book is actually a celebration. It invites its readers to drag their doubts out from under the rug, dust them off, recognize them as the gifts they are and voice them, confidently expecting resolution, as a scientist anticipates new enlightenment or a student questions a professor's argument. Doubts are not negatives but positives; not weaknesses but signs of strength; not preying forces of evil but tantalizing carrots enticing into new territory. Our response to our doubts separates the searchers from the scared. Rather than feeling slightly uneasy or downright overwhelmed by them, we can celebrate doubts, welcoming them with the anticipation of the first page of a new novel.

Doubts are signs of our health because they come from who we are, from our experiences. They are the grains of sand that irritate the oyster until the itching produces a beautiful pearl. They are catalysts, the factors in a chemical reaction that trigger substances to combine into new products. Doubts are springs that bubble up within us and will not be stopped. Even if capped or diverted, they burst out at inconvenient times like hiccups. Doubts are nudges and hints, sometimes more like shoves or blast-offs, but always the way our attention is captured and our mind expanded.

The Thesaurus lists "doubt" as the antonym of "faith" and "belief". Herein lies the problem to be corrected if doubt is to get a fair hearing. Firstly, there is a *difference* between faith and belief.   Religion scholar Wilfred Cantwell Smith (1916-2000) describes faith as our response to the experience of "something more". Beliefs are ideas, concepts or propositions concerning a religious tradition, formalized from the experience of faith and adopted by the individual or group.   Belief may be a *response* to faith, but faith is more than a set of beliefs. [6]

Faith is the experience of the individual, not a system of dogmas to be accepted. It is a way of seeing, a consciousness of another dimension. Belief centres on humanly developed propositions. Faith is a relationship of trust in, or response to, something experienced about which beliefs are fashioned. There is therefore a difference between the questions "What do you believe?" and "On what or whom do you set your heart?"   Faith and belief are not a package deal. It is possible to question or doubt particular beliefs as human descriptions of the ultimate, but still have faith in such a reality.

Any belief system - Buddhism, Islam, Hinduism - is a potpourri of centuries of cumulative tradition. Christianity itself has two thousand years of overlay on the man Jesus, his radical talk about love and justice and his untimely death.   Part of any such cumulative tradition is the stories, doctrines and interpretations that we label beliefs. In such belief systems you and I may live, having also experienced faith as a part of who we are — that desire for a relationship with, and/or trust in, something beyond ourselves, even if this is simply a gut feeling that we are not alone or that there is some point in being alive. This internal quality nudges us to look for and find meaning in this world, to experience life. What we are internally urged to seek is not locked into any infallible belief system.

Secondly, doubt is not, as the Thesaurus suggests, the antonym of either faith or belief. The opposite of faith is to be without the experience of faith. The opposite of belief is unbelief. Perhaps the best way to talk of doubt in relation to faith and belief is to see doubt as the awareness of a *discrepancy* between faith and belief. Doubts appear in religion, as in any system of learning, where there is a difference between what we are told to believe - taught as "truth" - and what we experience or intuit. Doubts occur when the belief system does not line up with our experience.

An anthropology professor left an exam paper for first year students with his secretary to be typed. A few moments later, the secretary entered his office. "Professor, I think there might be a mistake. I started typing this paper and then realized the questions are the same questions you set for last year's exam." The professor smiled and replied, "Yes, they *are* the same, but this year I've changed the answers!"

This is a parable about life. Answers to the questions about whom we are, who or what God is and what this world is all about, change with each generation. Answers are human attempts to understand and understanding is dependent on the particular situation of a generation, shaped by cultural, scientific, artistic, economic, political, ethical and other factors. In any generation, it is doubt that questions old paradigms and moves people to new answers.

Yet not all of us have been able to interpret them as such. Doubts are like earthquake tremors on the San Andreas Fault in California. Some folk live a lifetime ignoring the warning rumbles or even denying their existence. Others feel the shaking but refuse to act on their doubts, living a life of quiet desperation, hoping the rumbles will not loosen their traditional foundations enough to destroy them. Still others feel the tremors, acknowledge the chasm between experience and beliefs relentlessly growing wider and wider beneath them, but deal with it by moving to Florida. None of these are solutions. The tremors of doubt are warnings that not all is stable and secure in the belief foundations. Doubts must be acknowledged and creative efforts to "earthquake-proof" ourselves in that moment discovered.

"By whose authority do you do this?" the critics asked Jesus (Mark 11: 28). Doubts in religion are questions about authority, either the authority of one (or no) ultimate reality over another in interreligious debate or the question of one dogma over another in debates within a religion. Many indigenous religious traditions confer authority on the awesome activity of the natural elements. Jewish tradition sees the Law recorded in the Torah as authoritative. Muslims consider the Qur'an, Allah's revelation to Mohammed, the final authority. Early Christians saw their authority in the life and teachings of Jesus. Fourth century church fathers established creeds as authoritative for a church now linked to the Roman emperor. The reformers preached the authority of scripture as superior to any church declaration. Enlightenment thinkers endowed reason with authority, while twentieth century scholars chose science as authoritative. In the twenty-first century, we are more willing to allow our own experience to be authoritative for us. All these changes of allegiance to authority have been initiated by none other than doubt.

Year after year, the memory of Elvis Presley grows more mythical and revered. His drug addictions, problematic interpersonal relationships and the many defects that make up any human being, fade into obscurity in the legend that has replaced his person. Our selective memory enables us to forget the problems of the idols we create. What we do in religion is no exception to this. In the urge to hold up the saints as transparent perfection in the light of truth, we often ignore their encounters with doubt because we believe that such doubt is negative.

In actual fact, these heroes and heroines lurched from one crisis of doubt to the next, boldly proclaiming it, while growing more insightful with each new experience. Martin Luther's (1483-1546) doubts about the effectiveness and necessity of good works for salvation fuelled, along with other doubters, the Protestant Reformation. America's Elizabeth Cady Stanton (1815-1902) doubted the arguments that subjugated her and other women to males in the nineteenth century and bravely identified prevailing interpretations of certain biblical texts as validating this bias against women. Indian reformer Mahatma Gandhi's (1869-1948) doubts about the use of violence gave new models for the poor and outcast of India to protest their oppression. One ordinary American black woman, Rosa Parkes (1913-2005), somehow found enough courage to sit in the "white" section of the bus because she doubted that the colour of skin made some people superior. Her protest started what became the Civil Rights movement. Feminist theologian Mary Daly (1928-2010) accepted a prestigious invitation in 1971 to be the first woman to preach in the Memorial Chapel at Harvard University. From that pulpit, she voiced her doubts about patriarchal power in the church and ended by inviting all present to follow her in an "exodus-from-the-slavery-of-patriarchy" protest out of the sanctuary. Such stories will continue to emerge as long as there are people willing to doubt that religious dogma is written in cement, and to say so.

When does doubt arise? It appears when new experiences challenge previous thoughts, which may be every hour of the day. We are accustomed to seeing this process as a learning tool for life. A little girl stayed awake all night but no Santa came down the chimney. The next morning, her parents assured her that Santa used the back door. She considered this possibility until next Christmas, when she watched both chimney and doors. Finally her parents had to confess that Santa was a creation for a childhood period that she had now outgrown. The loss of the story was not devastating because her doubts had already prepared her for it.

Just as doubts about the Santa story initiated the little girl's move to new experience and understanding in the process of growing up, so it should be in the context of religion. Doubt becomes a moment of grace, an unpredictable and enlivening gift that assures us of the need to move. Doubt shows that work needs to be done on our life journey and grace fuels that work. We *may* deny the doubt by not allowing it access to our minds, or by filling our days and nights with so much clutter and noise that doubt is not heard. We *could* blame the devil for the doubt and thus shrug off any responsibility for it or ignore any message it may bring us. We *might* try to tell ourselves that doubt is weakness of faith. But in all these reactions, we are rejecting grace, that persistent gift of energy that pushes us forward into newness through our doubts and questions.

Doubts are not red flags indicating weakness, but auditors of our belief systems. This distinction is crucial. When successive bottoms fall out of successive doctrines that no longer fit our cultural and scientific worldviews, one does not "lose one's faith" by asking questions. For Paul Tillich (1886-1965), one of the great theologians of the twentieth century, it was possible for him to remain a theologian only by discovering this fact about doubt. He said:

The situation of doubt, even doubt about God, need not separate us from God. There is faith in every serious doubt, namely, the faith in the truth as such, even if the only truth we can express is our lack of truth. But if this is experienced in its depth and as an ultimate concern, the divine is present; and he who doubts in such an attitude is "justified" in his thinking. [7]

Granted there are cases where doubts about inadequate belief systems result in throwing the baby out with the bath-water. This usually happens when the doubter resides in a church or community that is inhospitable to doubt. Many who claim to be atheists and agnostics are products of belief systems that refused to encourage them to see doubts as gifts of grace. Such people may see the final surrender of their impotent belief system to unbelief, not as a personal victory but as a loss to mourn. When organized religion bewails falling numbers in churches and notes a surge of people outside the church calling themselves spiritual rather than religious, it needs to ask if these are the products of belief systems that refused to address new questions. To quote Tillich again:

> You cannot reach God by the work of right thinking or by the sacrifice of the intellect or by a submission to strange authorities, such as the doctrines of the church and the Bible. You cannot, and you are not even asked to try it. [8]

Doubts surface at the interface between faith experiences and the belief systems that have become static, stale or insipid, bogged down by unhelpful dogma or inadequate instruction. This interface, catalysed by doubt, is alive and dynamic, creating new richness of experience. Doubt acts with gentle nudges or gigantic prods. This book invites you to be attentive to this interface and see where God (however we envision that term) is in that movement. The following chapters examine negative mind-sets toward doubt, a negativity foreign to the saints of old; how doubts and our responses to them shape our life journeys and the persons we are becoming; and how we might relate to others who may not hold these same ideas, including people of other faiths. It suggests creative ways to address doubts so that we continue to push back barriers of inadequate belief systems that separate us from more authentic experiences of the Sacred.

These are not my ideas alone, conclusions navigated unaided. The permission to doubt has been a gift granted to me by a host of writers who have led me out of a narrow view into a broader view and keep cheering me on. This book is not just to read and swallow without chewing. Rather, as a thought stimulates the mind, the invitation is to begin one's own personal exploration around the subject; to affirm unique doubts spawned from individual experiences of background, culture, and knowledge; and to celebrate these doubts as leading towards new adventures. Religion scholar Joseph Campbell (1904-87) understood this:

> People say that what we're all seeking is a meaning for life. I don't think that's what we're really seeking. I think that what we're seeking is an experience of being alive, so that our life experiences on the purely physical plane will have resonances within our innermost being and reality, so that we actually feel the rapture of being alive. [9]

----

[4] Abelard, from *Sic et Non* (c.1120), quoted in Frederick Denison Maurice, *Mediaeval Philosophy, or A Treatise of Moral and Metaphysical Philosophy* (1870), 138

[5] Frank Rees, *Wrestling with Doubt: theological reflections on the journey of faith* (Collegeville, MN: The Liturgical Press, 2001), 1

[6] Wilfred Cantwell Smith, *Faith and Belief* (New Jersey: Princeton University Press, 1979) 12

[7] Paul Tillich, *The Protestant Era* (Chicago: University of Chicago Press, 1948), xiv

[8] Ibid., xiv

[9] Joseph Campbell, *The Power of Myth* (New York: Doubleday, 1988), 3.

Chapter 2.   A Great Tradition of Doubters

*"Therefore, since we are surrounded by so great a cloud of witnesses....
let us run with perseverance the race that is set before us."*
Hebrews 12:1

Life stories sometimes read like romance novels - handsome man meets beautiful woman and happiness reigns ever after.   But then, most times they do not.   Life is rarely a pattern of smooth transitions from one state to another.   Most of us are continually working on our lives and we may wake up one morning, unable to accept any longer the beliefs we once held, either because of their inconsistencies and inadequacies or because they no longer answer the questions of our lives.   It takes courage to struggle with issues of belief, staying in faith in *spite* of beliefs.

But such strugglers are part of a long column of people, an unbroken thread of resilient seekers wandering through history.   When some Christians today talk of simple gospels, simple faith and simple solutions, it is as if thousands of years of thought by both theologians and ordinary people who struggled to interpret the good news authentically for their time, never existed.   St. Augustine, Thomas Aquinas, Heloise, Theresa of Avila, John Calvin, John Bunyan, Florence Nightingale, Simone Weil, Paul Tillich, Rosemary Radford Ruether, John Shelby Spong, Marjorie Suchocki and countless others have wrestled with trying to understand who God is for their time.   At few points in their lives would they have claimed a theology all sewn up in a neat and simple package. Those people who proclaim a simple gospel actually don't want us to think for ourselves.

Struggling saints through history (I use this term for all seeking people) saw no need to tell it other than it was. Their autobiographies are alive with doubt, questioning, uncertainty, pain, but also with a sense of grace and an inexhaustible drivenness to know God.   Sometimes they prayed even though God seemed far away - or dead.   Dutch born Catholic priest Henri Nouwen (1932- 96) describes such a period in his journal:

> I have discovered how hard it has become for me to spend one hour in the
> morning simply being present with Jesus. I experience a certain nausea or

apathy that I did not have before.... a sort of spiritual fatigue, a state of luke-warmness in which I find it hard to know exactly what I feel, what I think, or what I want. It is like being a piece of driftwood on still water. Nothing seems to move, and there seems to be no way to get things moving again.... I do not feel depressed, just empty and somewhat different.....Well I am not panicky about it and try to stay in touch with Jesus. [10]

Sometimes joy surprised them with the clarity of sharp focus, but just as quickly zoomed back into fuzziness and doubt. No matter what new conflict presented itself, making havoc of their current belief systems, there was that faith that, through the opaqueness of a moment, more light would shine. Presbyterian pastor Frederick Buechner (1926-) writes:

God speaks to us in such a way, presumably, not because [God] chooses to be obscure, but because, unlike the dictionary word whose meaning is fixed, the meaning of the incarnate word is the meaning it has for the one spoken to, the meaning that becomes clear and effective in our lives only when we ferret it out for ourselves. [11]

When it seems easier to throw out everything at the first sign of conflict, these doubting ancestors who struggled through years of darkness because something lured them on, remind us of the great cloud of witnesses. Contrary to some Christian trends that name all doubt as negative, doubters are in healthy company. Autobiographies of such magnificent doubters are hardly hot sellers where people search for easy, sure-fire answers today, but we do well to discover the depth and power of such doubts and the creative newness of thought engendered in the process.

An anthology of doubters would take volumes. I have selected a sample from many periods and circumstances, both famous and not so famous. This selection is like a searchlight, roaming the night sky with no predictable pattern and no long pauses in any one place, sometimes hovering before moving on, sometimes returning for a second look and often missing altogether a section of the sky that should have been investigated. Such randomness however, strengthens the point that doubt has always been a creative persuader in every century and that true searchers have been the first to admit it. Jennifer Michael Hecht (1965-) said in her book *Doubt: a History*, "Once we see [doubt] as its own story, rather than a mere collection of shadows on the history of belief, a whole new drama appears ... [Doubters] tend to be more interested in what they have found than what they have lost. These figures are not howling in the abyss of the night; they're out there measuring the stars". [12]

Take stories in the Bible, for example. Sarah laughed in the face of the messengers from God who told her she would have children in her old age. Both she and Abraham doubted they could produce a nation. While the rest of the story concentrates on Abraham as the *father* of the nation, this outrageously impossible promise held a double significance for Sarah. Not only would she be the mother of a chosen people, but through pregnancy and birth, she would also find completeness in a patriarchal society where women's value depended on their ability to reproduce. Sarah's doubt was a normal reaction to a very human situation and Yahweh did not condemn her for it. In fact, Sarah was included in the mostly male listing of the great people of faith in the letter to the Hebrews (Hebrews 11:11). Faith and doubt were not incompatible here.

The tenacious psalmists were never backward in voicing doubts about God and God's activity, or lack thereof. Writing eloquently about a great and powerful God one day, they railed at God the next because God has withdrawn from the people. Faith and doubt hang in dynamic tension.

> How long, O Lord? Will you forget me forever?
> How long will you hide your face from me?
> How long must I bear pain in my soul,
> and have sorrow in my heart all day long? (Ps 13:1-2)

> My God, my God, why have you forsaken me?
> Why are you so far from helping me, from the words of
>   my groaning?
> O my God, I cry in by day, but you do not answer,
> and by night, but find no rest. (Ps 22:1-2)

> To you, O Lord, I call;
> my rock, do not refuse to hear me,
> for if you are silent to me,
> I shall be like those who go down to the Pit. (Ps 28:1)

However, the psalmists' cries seem tame compared with the accusations Job flung at God when he doubted what God was about.

> (God) has cast me into the mire,

and I have become like dust and ashes.
I cry to you and you do not answer me;
I stand, and you merely look at me.
You have turned cruel to me;
with the might of your hand you persecute me. (Job 30:19-21)

Job did not acquiesce when his friends told him to confess his wickedness for challenging God. Rather, Job believed in his right to question God's actions and dug his heels in for a long haul.

If I could only go back to the old days,
To the time when God was watching over me,
When his lamp shone above my head,
and by its light I walked through the darkness!
If I could be as in the days of my prime,
when God protected my home,
While the Almighty was still there at my side... (Job 29:1-4)

There was certainly no assumption that he had God's ear at all times:

If only I knew how to find Him,
how to enter his court,
I would state my case before Him
and set our my arguments in full;
Then I should learn what answer he would give,
and find out what he had to say. (Job 23:3-5)

The story of Job is the story of creative doubt. Strange and terrible things happened to him and his friends gave simplistic explanations, laying the blame on Job. Job rejected their answers. Their shallow solutions did not fit Job's experience of God. Job's faith in God, whoever God was, and his doubting of simple answers, made Job hold on, despite everything falling apart around him. Through this tension of both faith and doubt, Job entered into a richer experience of God.

Then Job answered the Lord:
"I know that you can do all things
and that no purpose of yours can be thwarted.
Who is this that hides counsel without knowledge?
Therefore I have uttered what I did not understand,
things too wonderful for me, which I did not know......
I had heard of you by the hearing of the ear,
but now my eye sees you". (Job 42:1-5)

Jesus was a Jewish layperson who doubted the religious rules and regulations of his day, especially as they applied to the poor. He saw people locked into rules they could not question and that disadvantaged them and denied their full humanity. Like the little boy who cried "naked", Jesus told the startled crowd they could pick grain and rescue their animals on the Sabbath. Soon he was deflating the accepted interpretation of the law right, left and centre. Because of his own experience of God, Jesus doubted these human constructs. He saw how they obscured a greater way of love. Those in authority tried to keep him quiet, but in the end there was only one way to silence him - by death.

In dealing with people, Jesus did not condemn those who questioned or doubted. While Jesus was harsh with Scribes and Pharisees who claimed to have all the answers in water-tight belief containers, he was always ready to encourage the genuine doubter. Many of these doubters were women, whose place in society did not permit them to challenge the male teachers of the day, yet Jesus allowed them to ask questions and air their doubts. Martha had no qualms about challenging Jesus when he arrived after her brother Lazarus had died. (John 11:21) The Greek woman who asked Jesus to cast out the evil spirit from her daughter would not be deterred by Jesus' response that his message was to the house of Israel. (Mark 7: 25-29). Thomas' request to see Jesus' wounded flesh before he would believe was treated with respect, not condemnation (John 20: 24-29). In fact, Jesus seemed to enjoy their challenges, often calling it evidence of their great faith.

What went on in those forty wilderness days at the beginning of Jesus' ministry and also in the garden at the end? While the biographers of Jesus sought to present Jesus as one who was confident in what he had to do, there are moments of doubt that were not erased from the stories. Jesus prayed in the garden that the cup might pass from him and cried out on the cross that God had forsaken him. Are we sure that there were not other unrecorded struggles for Jesus, periods of doubt and despair that were never shared with his followers or which later biographers did not wish to include? Research on the book of Mark, which suggests that Jesus did not necessarily understand himself as the Messiah, invites us to imagine how Jesus might have struggled with his own person and mission.

I wonder about Paul. Could his tirade against the followers of Jesus have been to squelch his own doubts? Did he attack so fiercely to cover up nagging questions he had about this man he persecuted? Whatever happened on that road to Damascus was sufficiently powerful to challenge Paul's constrictive religious beliefs and allow his doubts to lead to a new passion. The words spoken out of his vision, "Saul, Saul why do you persecute me?" could well indicate the culmination of his long-term dialogue with doubt.

The world of the early church was a scene of great fluidity of ideas. Diverse memories of Jesus vied for attention in the struggle to make sense of his life and death. In three accelerated years of ministry, Jesus had challenged prevailing interpretations of the Law, befriended tax gatherers and prostitutes, claimed intimacy with God and broken long-term Sabbath rules. In the dust and bustle around Jerusalem, he had so enchanted a group of unlikely people that they had given up their security to follow him. Despite their pleading, he plunged headlong into battle with the authorities and inevitably was killed.

In the aftermath of this whirlwind of intense life and premature death, everything at first seemed pointless to the demoralized group. When the women said that his spirit was still with them in some way, they knew it to be so in their hearts. The followers reflected on all that had happened in order to make coherent sense of Jesus' talk about love and forgiveness, about a coming reign of God that was also within them. Using both Hebrew and Greek symbols and categories to interpret the events, a theological "soup" brewed for the next three centuries, surging and receding, combining and re-combining, before out of it all, the creeds of the Christian church emerged, producing a fragile sense of stability and uniformity. What was the catalyst in this soup? It was doubt that disallowed theological certainty to rest until questions had been addressed and light, however temporary it might prove, had shone on the issues.

Many advocates today whitewash the early church, presenting it as a devout bunch of people, living, working and worshipping in blissful, loving harmony. Instead, much of the period was swamped with controversy. What was orthodoxy and what was heresy? As opposing theories were batted back and forth, doubts were not hidden but were the very centre of the discussions, catalysts from which a greater understanding would emerge. As will be seen later, not all doubts were given equal hearing because doubts challenge authority and authority is power. The theological soup had a liberal dose of political ingredients as well and the final creeds produced "winners" and "losers", "orthodox" and "heretic". Theological decisions made at the fourth century Church Councils were also influenced by the Roman Emperor as head of the church. Many doubters were silenced, sometimes by death. In this soup, there were other losers - women. Increasingly they were excluded from the places of leadership that they had earlier held in the community of faith, as the Greco-Roman patriarchal system headed by free, propertied males was incorporated into the emerging church's theology. It would take almost twenty centuries for those who doubted such structures to be heard to voice.

Saint Augustine of Hippo (354-430), who shaped much of Christian thought in his time, wrote an autobiography, not about his successes but about his struggles. His *Confessions* loudly acknowledge his companion doubt. Raised by a Christian mother, Augustine tells of the doubts that led him from the Christian scriptures to Cicero, to Manichaeism, to astrology, and finally into Scepticism. All belief lost and despairing of finding "truth", something drove him on, something to whom he wanted to give allegiance and in whom his soul sought rest. Call it doubt, call it grace, call it hints and traces of God, whatever the name, Augustine knew, intellectually and intuitively, that there was something to whom he should cling, even when he was not yet ready to cling. Despite his tortured faith, Augustine did not yield his integrity by refusing to face his doubts. These doubts became Divine fingers stretching out to him to beckon him to new experiences of trust. His doubts did not end there — all his life Augustine confronted new questions and new "heresies" to which he responded. Doubt, for him, was always a creative possibility, an initiative to search further.

No book, with the exception of the Bible, has been translated into more languages than Thomas a Kempis' (1380-1471) little book *Imitation of Christ*. This ordinary monk from the Low Countries of Europe wrote this essay on "the spiritual life" that has been read in every generation since. His actual life in the fifteenth century was routine and uneventful, yet an introduction to his book calls his writings the story of the human soul in which is caught up the reflections of countless other souls with the same yearnings, same strivings, same *doubts*, uncertainties and torments of unrest.

Another classic held sway in the Protestant world of the seventeenth century — John Bunyan's *The Pilgrim's Progress.* This allegorical book of simple scholarship is about a pilgrim who, despite all the obstacles he met to hinder his faith and resolve, pushes on. Bunyan (1628-88) had no claim to fame as a theologian in his time. He was, in fact, illiterate, until his wife taught him to read and write, enabling this personal story to be written. Bunyan reveals his doubts and despair in a continuing cycle of deliverance and uncertainty. It never occurred to him to hide his struggles, but rather he assumed doubt was a common experience, part of a continuing process from question to answer to question again. This is a far cry from today's personal "testimonies" that are triumphal stories of a spiritual life moving upward, ever upward. The popularity of Bunyan's book even into this century suggests he still has an audience!

When Danish theologian Soren Kierkegaard (1813-55) died, he left behind voluminous writings. His scholarship came out of a short life of forty years that struggled constantly with doubt. Kierkegaard believed he had inherited his father's guilt, the conviction of having committed the unforgivable sin. Doubting the complacency of the Danish church, he spent his life attacking it from within, calling the church from affluence to suffering and poverty for the Kingdom, to a faith that was to be lived not talked. Kierkegaard refused to set himself up as a model of the Christian life, going to the other extreme to deter people from imitating him. After nights of revelry, he would shed the playboy image and write for long hours to the detriment of his health. His biggest fear was that people should imitate him as a successful Christian and an authoritative figure free from doubt, rather than exploring faith and belief for themselves. In his book *Fear and Trembling*, he wrote:

> .... if things go wrong, then a doubter, even if by speaking he should bring all manner of misfortune upon the world, would still be far preferable to these miserable sweet-tooths who try and taste of everything and would cure doubt without being acquainted with it, and are therefore as a rule the immediate cause of outbreaks of ungoverned and unmanageable doubt. [13]

Frederick Schleiermacher (1768-1834), the father of post Enlightenment theology, inherited a world confronted with Enlightenment changes in cultural, scientific and philosophical world-views. Theology in the late eighteenth century was in disarray. Schleiermacher, raised in a strict but loving Brethren family, found intellectual freedom at University when confronted with doubts about traditional Christian thought. However, he refused to allow this doubt to negate Christianity altogether. He developed a way of thinking in his famous book, *On Religion: Speeches to its Cultural Despisers,* based on "feeling"' and the "experience of dependence" that could speak of faith for those who found theological beliefs bankrupt. By facing his own doubts, he addressed the collective doubts of his generation.

The experiences of women enjoy a wider hearing today, but this has not always been so. In each generation, however, a few women who stood up against subordination to males made it into the history books, to shine like blazing torches for a moment before the threatened hierarchy extinguished their light. Such was Elizabeth Cady Stanton, an extraordinary American woman raised within Calvinism and excluded from Union College because of her gender. When she attended a world anti-slavery convention in London, the women of the American delegation were not permitted to sit with the men on the floor of the conference. This experience made Stanton realize how much of this attitude towards women was argued from the Bible and, in the face of enormous opposition, proclaimed that the Bible had both suppressed women in society and also shaped their low self-esteem.

> When those who are opposed to all reforms can find no other argument, their last resort is the Bible. It has been interpreted to favour intemperance, slavery, capital punishment and the subjection of women. [14]

In the 1890's, Stanton, now over seventy, gathered together a group of educated women to produce *The Women's Bible* (she had studied biblical Greek since the age of eleven). By literally taking scissors to the sacred text, they collected together only passages that spoke about or included women, critiquing any passages that violated the rights of women or classed them as male chattel. They probed inconsistencies and exposed repeated blaming and classifying of women by men. When their experiences as women did not fit with what they were taught, they doubted the teaching and refused to be silenced. *The Women's Bible* was a best-seller. Stanton, however, was dissociated from the movement for the women's vote, of which she had been a founding leader along with Susan B. Anthony (1820-1906), because of her out-spoken challenge to male headship. These two women had shaped the movement in Stanton's kitchen, Anthony feeding Stanton's seven children while Stanton worked on Anthony's speeches.

A month before Nazi Germany fell in 1945, Dietrich Bonhoeffer (1906-45) was executed in Flossenbürg concentration camp. A pacifist Lutheran pastor, Bonhoeffer had denounced the inactivity of the German Lutheran church against Nazism and finally took part in a plot to assassinate Hitler. Bonhoeffer had been in the United States when war broke out, but returned to Germany rather than stay in safety to lead an underground seminary. He was arrested and killed. His classic book *Letters and Papers from Prison* is a journal account of his thoughts and experiences in prison. With the world gone mad around him, Bonhoeffer re-examined his church's teaching, writing in earnest from his own struggles with faith and doubt about a world that had come of age and needed a "religionless" Christianity. One by one, he replaced sacred cows of dogma with a new theology of costly grace, liberating the thinking of his generation. His writings inspired the Anglican Bishop of Woolwich, John A. T. Robinson (1919-83) to write *Honest to God*, a small book that spawned a huge controversy in Great Britain in the 1960's. Robinson was also facing his doubts about Christian teaching and was prepared to risk his career and security to share his thoughts with his era. His ideas, though threatening then, catalysed many people into opening the drapes over their doubts a little wider, including the American Bishop John Shelby Spong (1931-) whose books in the last few decades have liberated doubters forever — but more of him later.

The Second Vatican Council (Vatican II), stretching from 1962 to 1965, was instigated by the newly elected Pope John XXIII (1881-1963) in order to bring the Roman Catholic Church into the modern world, to open the church windows and let in some fresh air. This opportunity to doubt the status quo of Catholic teaching and tradition spawned a wave of new theologians asking questions. Henri Nouwen's writings within this new focus gave a new look to spirituality, solitude and the inner life across ecumenical boundaries, revealing a man with a remarkable grasp on a relationship with God. Yet Nouwen felt no need to protect this "spiritual superman" image in the eyes of his readers by presenting his life as free from doubt. Rather, he recorded his ongoing periods of doubt, trusting in their creative qualities.

In his book *The Road to Daybreak*, Nouwen discussed his decision to leave Harvard University to join the L'Arche Daybreak community in Toronto, a retreat for the intellectually handicapped. He struggled between outer voices urging him to stay in public life and inner voices saying, "What good is it to preach the Gospel to others while losing your own soul?" The book's theme is not "whereas once I was in doubt and despair, now I am whole". Nouwen tells of moments when he could no longer pray because of hurts and uncertainties and confesses ongoing feelings of anger despite noble thoughts and prayer. All is recorded unedited, the up and down moments of creative doubt calling to new life. Doubters have found great courage in Nouwen's words and his continuing disquiet does not tarnish respect from his readers. Rather, it encourages them to be honest about their own experiences and to share them with others. Nouwen did not expect this situation to end this side of the grave — his only consolation over the years was that the *desire to struggle* with mystery grew in intensity.

For many Catholic theologians, such as Hans Kung (1928-), Edward Schillebeeckx (1914-2009), Rosemary Radford Ruether (1936-) and Elisabeth Schüssler Fiorenza (1938-), who critiqued Catholic dogma during and after Vatican II, their pursuit of truth created great tension within their church despite the world wide popularity of their writings. Millions have seen their words as light in the pockets of darkness where doubts are hidden, as driftwood on an ocean for shipwrecked sailors. Readers recognize their own struggles within the writings of these theologians and find assurance that they are not alone. Yet both Kung and Schillebeeckx were censored by the church hierarchy and summonsed to defend their ideas. When Kung publically rejected the doctrine of papal infallibility in the late 1960's, the Vatican removed his license to teach theology in the *Catholic* faculty of the University of Tübingen, although he remained at that university as professor of ecumenical theology. For Ruether and Schüssler Fiorenza, lay women theologians trained within the Catholic Church, their struggle with dogma has been two-fold. As well as struggling with questions their male colleagues also challenged, they have been excluded both from ordination and positions of authority within the Catholic Church because of their gender.

The astute reader may have noticed something to this point - the scarcity of women as examples of courageous doubters. This is not a reflection on whether women doubt or whether women doubt *courageously*, but rather a comment on the socio-political patriarchal attitudes that have developed within Christianity, silencing women and their stories of doubt. Interestingly, after finishing writing this book on doubt in 1995, I realized how much of my own doubts as a teenager and young woman came from what the Bible or church said about women's roles and what they could or could not do. This realization evolved into a sequel book, *Why We're Equal: introducing feminist theology.*[15]

Women were important players in the early church. House churches were often headed by women of the household. Apostles sent out included many women whose names are recorded in early writings. However, by the time the later New Testament epistles (pastoral epistles) were written around 125 C.E., things had changed. The patriarchal structure of the Greco-Roman household had been adopted as the model for the socialization and organization of the Christian community. Patriarchy is not just a male-female issue or can be simply overcome by the use of gender inclusive pronouns. It is, by Schűssler Fiorenza's definition, "a socio-political system and social structure of graded subjugations and oppressions".[16] In such a structure, free, male, propertied heads of households sat at the top of the pyramid, with subordinate gradings of women, children and slaves. This structure, championed in Aristotelian philosophy, has been the dominant socio-political pattern of both Christian theology and western philosophy ever since, situating the male as powerful head above all others.

As this structure became the accepted norm for organization in the evolving church, women lost their equality and power in the community. The liberating words of the early Christian confession of Galatians 3:28, rejecting all hierarchies — "There is neither Jew nor Greek, male nor female, bond nor free" — lost its concrete egalitarian meaning and became "spiritualized" as something that would happen later "in Christ". It was only a matter of time before women were laden collectively with the sin of Eve. By combining a host of negative "bodily" qualities that women were supposed to possessed in greater quantity than men and by elevating the "spiritual" qualities supposedly possessed mainly by men, women were effectively demoted or removed in a male-dominated church. In words addressed to women by church theologian Tertullian (c.160-225 C.E.):

> Do you not know that you are each an Eve? The sentence of God on the sex of yours lives in this age: the guilt must of necessity live too. You are the devil's gateway ... the first deserter of the divine law: you are she who persuaded him whom the devil was not valiant enough to attack. You destroyed so easily God's image, man. On account of your desert — that is, death, even the son of God had to die.[17]

Part of the subjugation of women declared that women should not teach or preach. As a result, so little was written by women lest it be interpreted as such. All this leads to the tragedy that few records of the voices of our sisters exist over some nineteen hundred years of church history. From time to time, some writings and journals by religious women and mystics were preserved, but both these groups had been banished to the fringes of the institutional church. Fortunately, in the last fifty years, the feminist movement and feminist theology has recovered some of these lost voices not previously translated.

Feminist theologians seek a theology that affirms the full humanity of all women and their right to a voice in all public conversations. Feminist theologians come in many forms and convictions, but their common commitment is to the experience of liberation for women. Feminist theology has recognized the insidious harm caused by the refusal to allow healthy doubt where dogmas against women clash with women's own experiences. Feminist theology, therefore, *starts* with how women experience their world and suggests that any dogma which does not fit with women's experience must be treated with suspicion. Feminist theology allows women to doubt belief systems that cast all the players in male form and work in a patriarchal pattern of domination that excludes not only women, but others subordinated because of race, class, sexual identity or religion. Some women theologians have tried to work for change *within* the church but many others who have been denied their voice have left, not necessarily in joy but in sadness that the institution would not allow them to ask questions.

Feminist theology is a part of the broader spectrum Liberation theology that names doubt as central to theology with its idea of a "hermeneutic of suspicion". Individual context and experience is taken seriously and, if scripture and church teachings do not advocate a liberating and just experience in everyday life, one does not assume that one's *experience* is inadequate, but rather one questions the belief system offered. Under this rubric, oppressed people in the two-thirds world need no longer believe that their appalling poverty and powerlessness are the will of a God of love, allowed for their own good or for a heavenly reward. Instead, they search for forgotten themes in scripture about God's concern for the poor and oppressed. Many who find their voice through Liberation theologies discover an *angry* voice when they realize how a powerful few have forced them to suppress their doubts about certain interpretations of Scripture and authoritative claims of "superior knowledge".

I have mentioned very few doubters. Perhaps a Doubters Encyclopaedia should be written. However, these few may encourage the reader to take a second look at their doubts. These saints saw themselves as driven, tortured souls who would not rest until all was known, experienced, and lived. Their lives were, and are, a continuous process from points of doubt to hope on a journey. The commitment to risk this journey and the willingness not to block out doubt is the stuff of "sainthood". Without their personal honesty in the face of uncomfortable truth, we would not have their heritage of experience and openness to the nudges of God for as role models.

---

[10] Henry Nouwen, *The Road to Daybreak* (New York: Doubleday, 1988), 211

[11] Frederick Buechner, *The Sacred Journey* (San Francisco: Harper & Row, 1982), 7

[12] Jennifer Michael Hecht, *Doubt: a History* (New York: Harper One, 2003), ix, xvii

[13] Søren Kierkegaard, *Fear and Trembling* (London: Penguin Books, 1985), 135

[14] Elizabeth Cady Stanton, *The Women's Bible* (Seattle: Coalition Task Force on Women and Religion), vi

[15] Val Webb, *Why We're Equal: introducing feminist theology* (St. Louis: Chalice Press, 1999)

[16] Elisabeth Schüssler Fiorenza, *Bread not Stone* (Boston: Beacon Press, 1984), 5

[17] Tertullian, *On the Apparel of Women*, quoted in John A. Phillips, *Eve, the History of an Idea* (San Francisco: Harper & Row, 1984) 76

Chapter 3.   A Negative History of Doubt

Doubt comes in at the window
when inquiry is denied at the door.

Benjamin Jowett (1817-93) [18]

Doubts are natural, but their creativity or destructiveness depends on how we handle them, which depends on the cultural and religious baggage we bring to them, which depends on our ideas about authority and power. The way authority of knowledge has been used and abused in the history of Christianity is central to understanding how doubt has been regarded as negative.

Russian author Leo Tolstoy (1828-1910) observed from within his Russian Orthodox upbringing that, while educators were very careful about what they teach children in *school*, doctrines are taught within Christianity "that are incompatible with reason and knowledge". Once all this is indelibly stamped on the childhood mind to be believed, the religious educators then

> ... leave him alone to fathom as best he can the contradictions arising from the dogmas he has accepted and assumed as the undoubted truth. No one tells him how he can and should reconcile these contradictions. If theologians do try to reconcile them they only succeed in confusing the matter still further. And bit by bit a person grows accustomed (with strong support from theologians) to the fact that he cannot trust in his reason ... he must not be guided by his reason but by what others tell him. [19]

Authority is a key religious concept. According to the gospel story, when the chief priests and elders in the temple heard Jesus teach, they asked him, "By what authority are you doing these things and who gives you this authority?" (Matthew 21: 23) The question first in their minds was not whether his teaching made sense or nonsense, but from whom or where his authority came.

The first followers of Jesus believed that the authority for his message came from God, but after these followers had gone and there were no eye witnesses around to verify the stories, many differing views of the meaning of Jesus circulated. How did one decide what was "correct" since Jesus had written nothing down? For example, Gnostic believers claimed they had special "secret knowledge" handed down from the apostles to a special few, which set them in opposition to other communities that had grown up around various apostles. Against such "heresies", an "orthodox" position became established by the end of the fourth century, preserved both in the creeds of the church and the choice of writings to be included in the New Testament canon.

To prove *their* claim to authority, however, Gnostic Christians documented a genealogical line back to the apostles through which the secret knowledge had come. In challenge to this, an "orthodox" church father did the same and the idea of an "apostolic succession" to guarantee that the teaching had been passed on accurately came into being. At first this "orthodox" succession, recognized by the laying on of hands from one ecclesiastical figure to the next, was aimed at securing the authoritative content of the message. However, by the Middle Ages, when the church hierarchy had become an institution independent of ordinary people, this successive laying on of hands from bishop to bishop was said to transfer a special "indelible character", giving the ordained man a different state of existence to the lay masses. The authority of doctrine was solely in such hands and knowledge was power. Dogma was to be believed and obeyed, not questioned.

The various players in the Reformation around the sixteenth century challenged this state of affairs and, judging by the rate at which nuns and priests jumped over the walls of the monasteries to marry, there had been a considerable level of doubt smouldering under the surface of ecclesial souls. The reaction of the church hierarchy was to restate its authority through a series of declarations at the Council of Trent (1545-63) and doubting the teachings of the church remained a sin. The reformers, in turn, hailed the scriptures as their authority, but it was not as simple as that because few could read and the common people were still dependent on others to interpret scripture for them. Aware of the problems of multiple and competing scriptural interpretations, reforming leaders shored up "correct" interpretations in various denominational confessional statements. Authority of knowledge was still in the control of a few.

The Enlightenment of the seventeenth and eighteenth centuries became the grain of sand in the oyster of the institutional churches, both Protestant and Roman Catholic. Exciting new discoveries in science, art, world religions and the power of reason weakened the hold of old religious ideas and theology had not been the same since. No longer was the church the sole repository of learning and revelation. Doubt was able to flourish in all directions and catalyse new ways of thinking.

Frederick Schleiermacher, as we have already noted, made the "feeling of dependence" authoritative for the individual. This move allowed people to question the belief system handed down to them through the church and challenged by the Enlightenment and, like Cantwell Smith's distinction between faith and belief, centre their religious life on their own experience. Schleiermacher's move made possible the liberal movement in Christianity that flourished at the end of the nineteenth century and into the twentieth century. In this time of great optimism and faith in the ability of the human to progress towards knowledge and goodness, biblical research and critical study of texts blossomed, with a new openness to questions of scholarship hardly considered previously, questions which challenged traditional approaches to the authority of scripture. There seemed to be no limits. Everything was an open question.

Into the midst of this heady confidence of German theology broke World War 1. In the wake of disillusionment and defeat after the war, belief in the human ability to control its world was shaken. Despair and death forced people to look for some "authority" beyond themselves, some "certainty". Historically, periods of disaster have produced a rise in religious adherence to theologies where God's will is clearly and inerrantly defined and unquestioned. The period between the world wars was no exception and liberal thought was challenged both by neo-orthodoxy and fundamentalism.

The neo-orthodox trumpet was sounded by Swiss reformed theologian Karl Barth (1886-1968). Reacting to the bankruptcy he saw in liberalism with its search by humans to know God, he turned twentieth century theology upside down. Barth said that the question was not what humans thought about God, but what God had to say about humans. Thus any thinking that started with humanity rather than God - philosophy, psychology, historical criticism, piety - was unacceptable. Barth reversed what he saw as the uncertainties of humankind, to belief in the absolute certainty and sovereignty of God. He sounded to the embattled and betrayed survivor of wartime like a mother gathering distraught children to the security of her embrace. God acted in the revelation in Jesus Christ as told in the scriptures and humanity must believe and accept that action.

Barth's strong voice reflected his own journey from liberalism, but questions from human experience cannot be silenced by the loudness of an authoritative voice. Human questions are valid, as Job demonstrated, even if they are questions of and about God. The debate between Barth and liberalism is the ongoing debate between "the unchanging truth of the message" and the changing demands of the context or situation at any moment of history. Barth's emphasis on an eternal truth independent of human circumstances is what Paul Tillich calls "throwing the message at those in the situation, like a stone".[20]   While this may be effective in evangelical revivals and even more effective if expressed in aggressive theological terms, it does not take account of the need for theology to constantly correlate the message with the situation into which it comes.

Any claim to know authoritatively what are God's thoughts is open to the criticism made about Karl Barth that one has been privy to a look into "God's cards". When German New Testament scholar Rudolf Bultmann's (1884-1976) articles on the need to "demythologize" the biblical texts came in the wake of Barth's overwhelming rebuttal of any human questions, the suppressed doubts gushed out again, shaking the theological world. As Tillich said:

> Bultmann saved the historical question from being banished from theology...He showed that it cannot be silenced, that our whole relationship to the Bible cannot be expressed in paradoxical and supernaturalistic elements, not even if it is done with the prophetic power of Karl Barth. [21]

While Bultmann spawned a new generation of questioners and allowed for doubts to be examined again, Barth's writings held sway in the neo-orthodox tradition which offered a security needed at that period of history by sections of the church, a security of "certainty". Doubts were again seen as negative.

The other challenge to liberal thought was fundamentalism. This conservative evangelical tradition stemmed from the revivalist movements of eighteenth century Europe and America, offering an experiential alternative to the formality of confessional, liturgical churches. Fundamentalists wanted a return to what they called the "fundamentals". A series of booklets was launched under this name in America in 1909, protesting against the evils of liberalism, hence the title fundamentalists. This movement rejected evolution, scientific questions about creation, interest in comparative religion, and social gospel ideas. In many ways, their position took little account of changes from the Enlightenment.

In the fifties, there was a rift in the fundamentalist movement as some rejected its confrontational approach, anti-intellectualism and lack of social concern. The breakaway groups, whose most famous brother is Billy Graham (1918-), are generally called conservative evangelicals. Evangelicals and fundamentalists still share some basic theological ideas with varying degrees of militancy — the verbal inspiration of scripture, inerrancy and authority of the Bible, a stress on a personal faith experience of Jesus as Saviour and Lord, salvation only through Jesus, a commitment to converting the world to Christ and a mistrust of modern theology and critical interpretative methods of scripture analysis. I generalize here while realizing how problematic labels are. There are some within these groups who have moved beyond some of these positions, but for the most part, these categories characterize, to a more or lesser degree, the difference between their position and the liberal position they challenged. While Barth was not acceptable in these ranks during his life-time, changes in the evangelical position have now allowed his thinking access into this camp, or at least as a friendly near neighbour.

Fundamentalism and conservative evangelicalism offer certainty through unquestionable unchanging truth. They also offer for people in times of change a tight fellowship, held together by allegiance to common truths. It is attractive to those who feel alienated from society, but destructive for those who then become suspicious of claims of certainty once inside the group, since there is little room for doubt. Australian scientist Charles Birch (1918-2009), as one who left such a group, said:

> It is not at all clear that Fundamentalism provides an answer to the need for personal well-being of large numbers of people over a long period of

time. It can be quite damaging, unless it happens to be a stepping-stone to a more mature faith. [22]

History is important in order to help us understand our present in the light of our past. This historical diversion can serve to illustrate that over the centuries, ever since the time of Jesus, there has not been only one way of interpretation and understanding, one authoritative position, but many, ebbing and flowing, disappearing and reappearing. The life or death of a belief system has depended on how the authority of knowledge has been wielded as dominant power. Permission to doubt has always been inversely proportional to the power claimed through authoritative knowledge. Where a theological position claims the "truth" - authority of knowledge - and uses it to exert power of people, overtly or manipulatively, the ability to doubt is destroyed or severely weakened. Neo-orthodoxy, fundamentalism and conservative evangelicalism are strains of theology that still permeate Christian thought today and which deal in certainties, negating doubt.

What is today's theological climate? This question must include a consideration of the world-views under which we operate today. The Greco-Roman influence provided images for early Christianity with which to describe the events of Jesus' life. Anselm of Canterbury's (c.1033-1109) atonement theory — that God demanded a human sacrifice for human sin and sent his son instead — grew out of a medieval feudal society where the Lord of the Manor demanded punishment or death for a disobedient serf. The world view of the Enlightenment, with new understandings of science and human reason, allowed for more questioning of theology. Two World Wars and a Holocaust demanded a re-thinking of God's providence and plan. Today, we need to consider our own cultural and intellectual climate when we talk of theology. If it has anything to say to this generation, it must answer the questions the generation is asking, not questions asked in an earlier world-view that are no longer being asked. It must face squarely the doubts that arise from a disconnect between the thinking of fourth century Rome or the Middle Ages, or even twentieth century Europe, and address the realities of this age.

The word "postmodern" has been applied to our times, as opposed to what was called the "modern" world view or "modernity". The "modern" world view came into being with the Enlightenment and the Industrial Revolution. It was a move from limited technical capacities and understandings to the mechanistic age of science and technology. Science demonstrated a world running like a predictable machine that could be fathomed by the human mind. Such thinking forced theology to re-examine its ideas about God. Up to this point, God had been seen as divinely omnipotent, which in practice meant that God had created the world out of nothing, had established and was maintaining its natural laws and, from time to time, intervened (to varying degrees according to one's ideas about God's activity in everyday life) to accomplish divinely planned results. The efficacy of prayer was elevated to great heights with this understanding. In an era when death was the reality for most by the age of fifty and where plague and disaster were explained in external supernatural terms, God must be on your side and divine motives had to be found when tragedy occurred.

The emerging view of science and a mechanistic world was problematic for theology because it left little for that sort of a God to do. How was God the "cause" in such a world? Was God the driver of the machine, guiding and steering everything within the world and able to override laws God had, in fact, created? Or did God set the world in motion at creation, wind it up, then leave it tick away like a clock forever without interference from without? Or was God a God of the gaps, the explanation for anything where science let us down or withheld secrets? Most threatening of all, could we do without a God altogether — was there still a role for such a God in the world? The question of questions, the nudging doubt was, of course, did God even exist or was all this a figment of our imagination, a need created for powerless people in a scary world?

What we call the postmodern world view moved beyond this modern view. Just as new scientific ideas were heralded in the modern era, evolving scientific ideas have played a major part in the postmodern era. I will highlight briefly some of the changes in thinking. Until the 1960's, positivist and empirical views of science had held sway, views that assumed the world could be fully described from factual data, observed by experiment through our senses. Objective scientific theory could be built up from these observations, not influenced by subjective or personal bias or interpretation. Scientific knowledge was proven knowledge of how the world objectively *is*.

But the foundations of such authority started to shake. Scholars became interested in the philosophy of science. They stood back from the assumptions which had held sway for years and asked questions about them.

1. Was science as objective as everyone thought? Did not the scientist come to research with her own questions to be proved or disproved? Was not the selection of what hypotheses would be examined a "subjective" valuation?

2. If a theory was proved, was this "absolute truth" or was such truth rather the best available constructs from clever minds which advanced scientific knowledge beyond a previous inadequate "truth"? Thus if a scientific theory was "falsifiable" i.e. could be shown to be inadequate under testing, did it actually became more valuable scientifically because its demonstrated inadequacy led the way to greater knowledge?

Taking note of this "falsification" approach, Thomas Kuhn (1922-96) realized that any theory was part of a much more complex structure of things and did not stand or fall by itself. Theories emerged from the scientific world view of a particular time, with its set of laws agreed on by the scientific community. Any testing of a new theory was done in light of this mutually accepted theoretical structure which Kuhn called a "paradigm". In his classic book *The Structure of Scientific Revolutions*, [23] Kuhn showed how science has been a succession of revolutions when an existing paradigm is abandoned in favour of a new one incompatible with the old one. The revolution occurs when the old paradigm no longer adequately accommodates new findings. Anomalies mount up until a crisis occurs and scientists are forced to adopt a new paradigm of scientific thought.

We have currently watched a Kuhn paradigm change with the new physics. The mechanistic model of the universe has been replaced by an organic model, less deterministic, more organic and more subjective. In the old model, the whole universe could be reduced to objects or matter, moved only by locomotion from without. There was no consideration of the inner capacity of an object for self-movement, or any thought of the internal effects of one object on another. Quantum physics, however, in its search for the smallest element of "stuff", has focused, not on the "stuff" as an object, but the activity or "event" in which the stuff takes part, an event that involves not just external influences pushing or pulling, but also subjective or internal activity as well. Charles Birch described it this way:

> There is a "within" of things which is what things are in themselves and to themselves. The stuff of the world is "feelings" or relations clothed in "emotion". Subjectivity is everywhere in nature. [24]

This postmodern approach to science, where science itself recognizes the limits of the mechanistic model, has changed our world-view. Science is identifying the subjectivity of matter within itself; "feelings" and self-determination for more than just humans and higher animals; and the importance of the relationships between things, of being affected by others but also effecting others. Rather than a machine directed from an outside force, whether by God or universal laws, the world is a living organism, all parts mutually interdependent and influencing each other. Relationships between both people and nature where both are experiencing subjects are important, rather than some parts of the universe treating other parts only as objects.

What does this have to do with doubt? Surprisingly, quite a lot. As we have seen, Christianity and culture (world view) are closely interwoven. Although Christianity can challenge culture, it is also formed by culture to the extent that any belief system to be a "living faith" must answer the questions and concerns of people in their situation and in their cultural language. Christ is not good news if the problems from which Christ saves us are not the problems about which people are concerned. Good news to the poor of the two-thirds world is not to suffer one's lot and await heavenly rewards if the Bible *also* talks of God leading people out of slavery in the Exodus story. The earth says it is not "good news" being poisoned, polluted and destroyed just because the creation story in Genesis commands humans to dominate the earth — Genesis *also* records God calling creation very good. Women say it is not "good news" to submit to a husband who batters her unconscious when Jesus demonstrated in his life the equal worth of men and women.

For Christianity to be a living faith, it must answer the questions of the postmodern world view. It must, like science, make paradigm changes. A paradigm change in religion comes about when prevailing dogmas no longer explain our experiences in the world, when creative doubt challenges inadequate theology in light of a new world-view. The emergence of many new theological approaches in our postmodern world is indicative of the realization of the need for change. However, as in any other period in the history of Christianity where there has been a major change in world-view, there are some who drag their feet, claiming that Christianity is unchanging — the same yesterday, today and forever.

Scientific paradigm changes need consensus by the scientific community that the old paradigm is no longer adequate. But Kuhn reports that such changes are not always clear-cut. Some scientists continue using the old paradigm, working independently on the fringes with no correspondence with the mainstream since their basic premises are incompatible. It is the question of authority again. They still claim authority for their old paradigm and operate within that structure, despite the moves the rest of the world has made.

Eventually in science, an old paradigm will be falsified by scientific method and will die. It is not so clear-cut in religion. There is no agreed on "theological method" as a final authority by which one tests all theories. That may sound strange. Surely God as expressed in Jesus Christ is authoritative for Christianity? Were it that simple! The existence of countless denominations and sects demonstrate that it is not. The authority of God has been claimed by every pope, every charismatic leader generating a new sect, every mystic in contact with God and every TV evangelist through the "correct" reading of scripture. All of these claim authority through the same God, the same Jesus and the same scriptures.

Doubt is about challenging prevailing authorities and paradigms. As I said before, the ability to doubt is inversely proportional to the strength of the dominant authority. Here we finally get back on track about how negative attitudes to doubt emerged. When the world-view of the Enlightenment challenged ecclesiastical authority, people experimented with their new freedom, trusted their experience, were open to creativity and tested their thinking against a plurality of ideas. Schleiermacher's emphasis on personal experience as authoritative for faith, "a feeling of dependency", allowed people to stay in their churches without denying the changing world around them. This freedom of thought was nipped in the bud by post-war theologies which returned authority to a particular reading of scripture, suppressing doubt once more. The writings of Dietrich Bonhoeffer, Paul Tillich, John A. T. Robinson and others led in the sixties to the "Death of God" movement when traditional images of the Divine no longer worked for peoples' experience of the world and new ways of thinking about God emerged.

Today, all the old "gods" are being challenged, whether they are doctors, lawyers, scientists, academics or priests, opening up access to new creative ways of thinking not possible in past paradigms. Once again, human experience (subjectivity) has been recognized as authoritative, not something to squelch as inadequate or flawed. We now admit that all theologies over the centuries have been entwined with the human experiences of those expounding them. The questions with which great thinkers have personally struggled become revolved or explained in their emerging theological ideas. Saint Augustine struggled with his personal inability to control his sexual desires and, from that experience, the doctrine of original sin was shaped — something must be innately faulty in the human being, passed on through sexual intercourse from the tainted sin of Adam. Martin Luther struggled with an inability to feel God's forgiveness despite the lengths to which he went to do penance, hence his revelation from the book of Romans that forgiveness had to do with faith and grace, not works. Contemporary Feminist, Liberation and Progressive theologies all started from human experiences of authoritative teaching that did not fit what one knew and felt, theologies that kept people oppressed, whether women, poor people, or laity who simply must believe the doctrines. They all reflected on their experiences and found new interpretations of scripture that liberated them rather than being bound to outdated, culturally limited doctrines as absolute "truth" for all time. Doubters are, therefore, in excellent company.

Yet in the midst of such creativity and openness, there is always opposition. Whether it be from the Religious Right, special revelations to Pentecostals, or Papal encyclicals; whether authority is claimed through church tradition or divine signals, it is all the same move despite its garb, the oppression of individual thought and experience (and thus doubt) through power claimed because of authoritative control of interpretation. That knowledge can be authoritative is not at question here — we *all* choose loci of authority from which our own knowledge develops. But when such authority becomes "power over" and used to control or suppress individual creativity and thought, it becomes destructive.

Such oppressive "power over" includes the power of naming. Winners can name losers in relation to themselves and those with power can describe the masses as they please.   Thus when all Muslims are called terrorists, feminists are called fanatics, people acting for social justice are called communists and those who challenge fundamentalist doctrines are called secular humanists, the ones doing the naming are classifying the "other" in relation to themselves however they wish, always placing themselves as the superior stance.   If one can name the other as enemy or as inferior, it is easier to justify aggression towards, or dismissal of, that other.

In the same way, people's attributes can be named either positively or negatively. A doubter can be a person of great creativity and adventure who challenges the status quo and pushes knowledge forward, or a person with a weakness of spirit or intelligence, depending on the context in which the label is applied.   Those who believe God is active in the world and in individual experiences can name doubt as creative nudges from God. Those who see doctrines as eternal propositions to be accepted by faith without question name doubt as a weakness. In the latter scenario, doubt is said to have nothing to do with the validity of a belief system or the need for a paradigm change — it is a problem with the *doubter*. It is either a sign of internal spiritual weakness and lack of faith or a sign of the doubter's lack of fortification against the external attacks of a devil. Either way, the doubter is to blame.

Frances Ridley Havergal (1836-79) spent her short sickly life evangelizing all those around her.   She wrote emotive hymns of commitment and surrender such as "Take my life and let it be", "Who is on the Lord's side?", "Truehearted, wholehearted, faithful and loyal" and "Lord, speak to me that I may speak". She also wrote a devotional book *Kept for the Master's Use.* She was not, however, "immune from the trials of the flesh, nor the human spirit", her biographer says — "Like anyone else, she too was plagued from time to time by doubts and impatience".   Francis is quoted as saying:

> I had hoped that a kind of table-land had been reached in my journey, where I might walk awhile in the light, without the weary succession of rock and hollow, crag and morass, stumbling and striving, but I seem borne back into all the old difficulties of the way, with many sin-made aggravations. I think the great root of all my troubles and aggravations is that I do not now make an unreserved surrender of myself to God; and until this is done I shall know no peace. [25]

While admitting to doubts, Havergal could only see them as *her* fault, her lack of total surrender to God in an already devotion-filled life. Rather than exploring her doubts, she struggled to be more obedient and submissive.

Such an abusive attitude to doubt parallels the abuse by a dominant power of women in rape and domestic violence and of children in incest and child molestation. Not only does society want to blame the victim for the behaviour, but the victim herself is indoctrinated to accept the violation as her own fault. Her own authority has been negated and she has internalized the belief that other superior authorities substitute for hers. In child abuse, the parental authority figure makes such claims without question. In marriage, society has long encouraged a subordinate role for women and this inequality is still promoted by conservative religion, albeit in more seductive descriptions of a woman's correct role. While our postmodern world view challenges patriarchal attitudes of domination and legislates against it, religious traditions who claim their doctrines as unchanging truth continue the patriarchal structures of theology and condemn those who challenge their abusive tendencies.

With physical abuse, those not subjected to it, or else indoctrinated to accept it, cannot understand how such power relations can be tolerated by the victim. In the same way, those who have not been subjected to a theology that victimizes by blaming the doubter for doubting cannot understand why one does not challenge the authority and refuse to take the blame. In a patriarchal marriage relationship, women surrender authority to the male and thus open themselves to possible abuse if such authority becomes "power over" the other. In patriarchal theology, individuals surrender their own experiences, thoughts, and doubts to another authority that may use this authority as "power over" individual creative thought, victimizing the doubter.

When doubts about doctrines, such as a virgin birth, a bodily resurrection, an infallible Pope, a blood sacrifice to appease a righteous God, enter your mind because they do not fit with reason or your experience of life, it is abuse to be taught that your doubt is your sin, your weak faith or your eternal damnation. To accept such abuse by submerging doubts before a sea of victorious Christians who seem to have no problem believing is evidence that you have internalized the blame and need help to break free.

Negativity towards doubt rests on how we interpret scripture. In the early days of church history, Bible stories were interpreted both as allegorical and didactic stories, as well as factual accounts. The church fathers decided which meaning would be the accepted one for the church — "orthodoxy" versus "heresy". These categories have moved over the centuries as some ideas labelled heresy have resurfaced as convincing arguments for later times. The Reformation fathers designated scripture as the norm of authority, rather than an official church interpretation, yet they also realized the problem of many individual interpretations of scripture. Some reformers argued for a "common sense" reading of scripture as the correct way to interpret the text now that the scriptures were translated for all to read and not just in Latin for theologians. Luther selected a theme for the gospel message, "justification by grace through faith", and thus assigned less authority to sections of scripture that did not enlarge on this theme. He had little time for the letter of James since it emphasized works as well as faith. Reformer John Calvin (1509-64), on the other hand, made all scripture the authoritative word of God and worked hard to interpret every part of scripture as from God.

The successors of the Reformation dealt with the problem of multiple interpretations by establishing authority through confessional statements accepted as foundational truths. Some later declared scripture to be literal, inerrant, infallible and not open to question. When scripture or confessional creeds are interpreted literally as inerrant for all times, a Christian with a "strong faith" must never be shaken or dismayed, but simply "believe", even when experience or science or any external knowledge disagrees with doctrine. Doctrines are not seen as limited products of their time and open to re-interpretation in successive cultures, but eternal truths authenticated by a literal understanding of scripture as interpreted by approved scholars with the authority of correct knowledge. To doubt these interpretations is to question not only the scholars, but — God "himself". Doubt is a condemnation of the quality of one's faith, one's ability to believe unquestioningly and therefore one's salvation. Discrepancies between doctrines and our own experience are simply proof of the depravity of our human wisdom.

Doubt, therefore, is something to overcome with much prayer and confession. Doubt is good value in a testimony about what God has rescued us from, but such doubt can only be acknowledged in retrospect, after victory over doubt has been won. In this scenario, doubt is not a creative adventure but a guilt trip. To maintain a place within the fellowship of the church community as a doubter, one has to live in a state of intellectual dishonesty, unable to make sense of the rules and interpretations of the authority, but blaming oneself for the predicament. Of course, this fits right in with teachings about original sin, where we are condemned for something with which we were supposedly born and from which we cannot escape.

Such is the evil of naming doubt as personal weakness rather than creative nudging. Our rugged ancestors in doubt, with their healthy and cavalier approach, shouted to both God and the world that they would not be thus manipulated. Their biographies show that negativity towards doubt has not always held sway in history but stems instead from the abuse of authoritative power that makes the doubter a victim. The road to recovery from such oppression may be long, but the initial hurdle is to recognize what has happened as unhealthy and start forward.

Feminist theology throws light on another aspect of how the naming of doubt as negative is maintained. Doubts about the natural inequality and thus subjugation of women have existed since time immemorial — we can trace the rise and fall of feminist protest in history as individual women or small groups of women found their voice in male-dominated societies and spoke out. [26] But the protests were silenced because women were isolated from each other and not in positions of power where their corporate voice could be sustained against the male hierarchy. Nor was there a written history of feminine role models who had protested before them from which to draw affirmation. Male authority voices have validated pyramidal structures with men on top as the unquestioned norm throughout history and the public silence of women's voices has forced those who personally questioned the system to believe such discontent was simply their problem. When Florence Nightingale (1820-1910) raged to her good friend and colleague, Oxford scholar Benjamin Jowett, about how Victorian families "murdered" their daughters by keeping them sewing in the drawing room and not letting them accomplish any important work, Jowett simply assumed this was a problem unique to Nightingale and advised her not to quote this personal experience in her theological writings as that would lessen the weight of what she said! [27]

I can remember as a teenager watching my mother spend hour after hour making beds, cooking meals, washing dishes, only to go to bed and redo it all the next day. At the time, I was being encouraged to study hard and earn distinctions, yet always with the understanding that, once I fell in love and married, a good Christian woman would count all such educational achievement as dross for the sheer privilege of repeating what my mother was doing - making beds, washing dishes, "as unto the Lord". Patriarchal Christianity had somehow elevated drudgery to nobility for women, throwing in guilt by equating any doubt and discontentment about this with selfishness and pride. I can remember the chills of fear inside me that I had thought such sinful thoughts, my consternation compounded because I could not clear my mind of envy and frustration that my male peers, earning B's and C's to my hard-won A's, would be the next generation of professors while I washed and ironed, perhaps for one of them.

At that time of my life, the mission field seemed very attractive, the one area of opportunity for women where permission to follow one's dream for adventure and career (you could use the more spiritual word "call") was given and even deemed noble. In such a setting, a woman was valued for doing "the Lord's work" through her career, while still able to be a wife and a mother by relinquishing home and child-care duties to local household help. No wonder many stay-at-home wives and mothers worked so hard in missionary unions, baking and sewing to make money to send to these overseas sisters. Through them, ordinary women could live vicariously their own aborted dreams.

The feminist movement of these decades took on steam only when women gained enough voice in the public arena and academy to challenge the authority of men, the patriarchal norm, and share their experiences together. Early feminist theologians, searching for a name for the theological insights emerging as women talked together and discovered similar feelings, suggested "yeah-yeah" theology (not of course as a serious proposal), that gasp of identification that escapes when solitary doubts are named and claimed by more and more, rising into a loud unified shout.

When I recall the struggles I personally had with doubts in a theological environment where doctrines could not be questioned, the enforced isolation comes most vividly to mind. I could spot so many inconsistencies in the dogma but no one else seemed to see the problems or, if they did, they too were suppressing their doubts in order to be accepted by the group. In my university setting in the sixties, those offering water-tight arguments in my particular Christian organization were the scientists trying to marry religion and science rather than the theologians who were, at that time, all reading Bishop Robinson's *Honest to God*. As an undergraduate science student, this did little to relieve my sense of inadequacy because of my doubts. Not only did these leaders seem to believe everything with clarity and ease and claimed they could demonstrate such doctrines compatible with their scientific method, their certainty seemed to be rewarded with visible signs of God's blessing - miraculous parking spaces, fortuitous phone calls and impeccably timed bible verses.

When finally in middle age I plucked up courage to throw caution to the wind and expose myself to the evils of a university religion department where I would lose my faith as many told me, I discovered there were others who had asked my questions, many in fact rather famous theologians. My previous isolation from such thinkers had been achieved through claims of heresy made against all those outside the authoritative theological position held by my group. When I had absorbed a smattering of biblical criticism in my religion classes, about which I was intensely excited, I shared my new discoveries with someone in my Christian group who worked with an organization promoting bible reading. It was like poking a stick into an open clam shell — nothing closed up as fast as his face. After a few moments of pregnant silence he said, "Never mind, I'll pray that you will find your faith again" and the discussion was over.

While mainline churches may be more receptive today towards doubt and questioning, a new brand of Christianity has emerged, imitating American culture with its pre-packaged, instant gratification attitude to life — gain without pain or strain. Such a world view demands everything to be accessible or achievable by following a set of easy, guaranteed instructions. There is something slightly unnerving about a society that cannot add a column of numbers without a calculator, does not know what to do with raw corned beef if there is no pastrami at the deli, does not know how to peg out wet clothes if the dryer goes on the blink and cannot function when the computer goes down. Even dieting requires no effort - you simply wrap some garment around you and lose weight while you sleep.

Why are most best sellers today "how to" books"? Because it is easier to imitate success than experiment for yourself. No one will buy a diet program if the possibility of failure is mentioned — fine-print such as "individual results may vary" protects against any law suits. Anything that involves prolonged commitment or has no absolute guarantee is suspect. Contemporary culture aims to eliminate all need for risk, personal learning experiences and the possibility of failure by offering guaranteed information on how to emulate those who have succeeded, with success measured in material terms.

This fantasy world of vicarious experiences is epitomized in television. Unpaid bills can be transcended by watching the lives of the rich and famous. Feelings of powerlessness in the work-place vanish by immersing oneself in violent TV battles or through confrontational computer games that allow you to win. Difficult family relationships are escaped through the erotic stimuli of soap opera characters whose clothes never crush and whose babies, if they choose to have them, never cry. Who needs to go to Africa when big game animals stroll across our screens minus the flies and dust? Why read a book and have to imagine its characters when Hollywood will visualize them for you in living colour? Even in politics we expect instant, painless results. Presidential nominees promote simple recipes for national solutions and people vote for the most believable or most charismatic. We quickly lose faith if instant results don't appear. In international affairs, money or arms lurch in to solve conflict, rather than attempting the more time-consuming, more difficult and less popular methods of conciliation and cooperation.

Much of television Christianity with its glitzy mega-churches has adopted this cultural epidemic, offering a pre-packaged trinity of salvation, success and security. There is no need to struggle with doubts now because there is no need to think for yourself. Anyway, how could one doubt the God they preach when the proven success of the religious formulae is embodied in the TV evangelist - confidence, wealth, glamour, smiling countenance, wealth, power, influence, wealth, assurance, wealth, instant results, success, wealth, wealth......?

Such direct marketing of religion aims at eliminating doubt. While the gospel message was initially for Jews, it moved to mass marketing when the good news was later proclaimed to everyone — "Go and make disciples of all nations" (Matthew 28: 19). People listened, argued, mumbled together and meditated about the stories. Some, like our friend doubting Thomas, needed proof to believe; some, like Peter, vacillated back and forth; others like Paul responded in an instant when the message finally filled his need. Success or failure was not measured by an immediate response when the music played at the end of the sermon. Rather, the Spirit of God was allowed to work over unlimited time. The good news also came in many different shapes and sizes in the early days of the church — Paul chided congregations for squabbling about allegiances to Apollos or Paul or whoever had the only "true package".

Today's popular direct marketing of religion, on the other hand, is totally controlled and aimed at identified types of people to obtain optimal results. Those not likely to respond are not targeted. The product is obtainable only through the particular advertiser and the marketer controls the product until delivery. Rather than build up the product image over time, with opportunities to examine the product before purchase, the direct marketer requires an immediate measurable response in the limited time frame through a special offer, often without seeing or touching the product itself. The three key criteria of direct marketing are (a) a definite offer made to the customer which (b) contains all the information necessary to decide, and which (c) provides a purchase response method e.g. a mail in coupon, a phone number etc.

TV style evangelism exemplifies the principles of direct marketing. A pre-packaged solution-product, designed to appeal instantly to those targeted, is aimed at audiences through TV, popular Christian literature and fast-growing mega-churches. Bob Stone's seven step formula for success in direct marketing reflects the blueprint used by some of today's faith peddlers.

1. Promise the most important benefit in the headline.

2. Immediately enlarge on this to build up interest fast.

3. Tell the client specifically what they will get, intangibles as well as tangibles.

4. Back up your statements with proofs and endorsements, third party testimonials from satisfied customers.

5. Tell the client what he/she might lose if they don't act. This overcomes human inertia by implying what may be lost if action is postponed.

6. Rephrase your prominent benefit in the closing off- this provides a prelude for asking for action and intensifies the listener's desire to have the product. The stronger the benefits, the easier it will be for the buyer to justify an affirmative action.

7. Demand action now. Once a letter is put aside, you lose the battle of inertia. [28]

Any marketing promotion can emphasize one of three features - the product itself, the advantages of the product over other products, or the benefits the customer will enjoy. Pushing the benefits produces the most sales. Benefits can be immediate (obvious), or ultimate (related to the consumer's feelings or values). The benefit equation is:

BENEFIT divided by PRICE = VALUE

The value of the product is thus determined by what's in it for me compared with what I have to pay for it.

The benefits equation preached in Christianity has varied over history. The price was high in the early days of persecution but the benefits for eternity from a martyr's death were great. After the apostles had all died, martyrdom became the highest honour in the community, above bishop or teacher or prophet. Ignatius, the third Bishop of Antioch (35/50-98/117), went eagerly to Rome for his martyrdom. To cling to life and material benefits were values furthermost from his mind. By the Middle Ages, however, martyrdom was hardly touted as a benefit for bishops in the Roman church. By virtue of their ordination, they were considered next to God in power and authority, with material benefits at a premium - wealth, excesses, influence. The price in inconvenience paid for such a lifestyle was negligible. Even celibacy was in name only. Everyone wanted in.

For writer Alexander Solzhenitsyn (1918-2008) in communist Russia, the price for writing about justice and oppression was high, the material and physical benefits very low. Few stood up for the faith, not seeing any value in such defiance. Yet for Solzhenitsyn, the awareness that God was present with him in his suffering was the shining point, the ultimate benefit of existence, the only thing that made sense in his world of oppression and despair.

Why is popular TV evangelism so successful today? Because it has identified what our culture values most and what it fears most and is marketing both of these as benefits of Christianity. The benefits are all self-oriented - health, money, security, approval, excitement, power, fulfilment, freedom, identity, escape, possessions and sex. These are obtained through miraculous Disneyland-style experiences that bypass struggle, work and thought. Such benefits are promoted as God's "reward to the faithful" and claimed through such texts as "Ask anything and everything, and you will receive" (Matthew 7: 7). Not much information is given, just enough to get a response to the package within the time frame to complete the deal. This brand of Christianity promises all these earthly benefits, with eternity as well. There is no high price, except perhaps a sizable donation; no persecution, no hardship, no social protest. Instead, God commits the divine self to *us* and waits like the genie of the lamp for our orders "in the name of Jesus".

No wonder people respond to those who propose such a religion. Psychologist James H. Leuba (1867-1946) wrote:

> As long as [people] can use their God, they care very little who he is, or even whether he is at all. God is not known, he is not understood: he is used - sometimes as a meat-purveyor, sometimes as moral support, sometimes as friend, sometimes as an object of love. If he proves himself useful, the religious consciousness asks no more than that. Not God, but life, more life, a larger, richer, more satisfying life is, in the last analysis, the end of religion. The love of life, at any and every level of development is the religious impulse. [29]

Where is doubt here? Nowhere. It is not even in the equation, not part of the package sold, even in the small print. In fact, if you buy this package, complete with simple instructions, doubt will disappear, because the promised results are quality controlled, assured and tested. You have purchased something proven perfectly compatible with the value system of the average American and fully secured. The money-back offer will, of course, never be claimed, because to doubt the effectiveness of the package is to doubt the effectiveness of the genie Spirit whose contract is to fulfil every desire. "If you ask anything in my name, I will do it" (John 14: 14) is no longer an offer to be co-creators with God through our lives, but rather our divine credit card with unlimited purchasing power.

Doubt in this scenario becomes the devil. By personifying doubt as the opposing force to the belief package, doubt is not personal weakness of faith, but taking one's eyes momentarily off the glittering deal, thus allowing an attack to ensue. Anything that raises questions or hints at uneasiness about the efficacy of the religion package is unquestionably the devil at work who then has to be removed immediately, without listening to what the devil might say. What brilliant manipulation. *God* can speak at any time to charismatic leaders, but only the *devil* speaks to the followers. Dogmas proclaimed by the spiritual authorities are challenge-proof, but doubts verbalized by hearers condemn them as gripped by the devil. If doubt is the devil's weapon against the authority of the preacher, doubting individuals must be exorcised so as not to endanger the channel of communication to the community through the proper authority. In actual fact, it smells of the fear of reprisal the nodding crowd expected from the emperor should they speak their doubts.

No wonder the sixteenth century writer of these words ever had his own TV show — his benefits wouldn't sell!

> My God I love Thee.
> Not because I hope for Heaven thereby.
> Nor yet because who love Thee not-
> Must die eternally.
> Thou, o my Jesus, Thou didst me upon the cross embrace,
> For me didst bear the nails and spear
> And manifold disgrace;
> Why, then why - o blessed Jesus Christ,
> Should I not love Thee well?
> Not for the hope of winning Heaven
> Or of escaping Hell;
> Not with the hope of gaining aught,
> Nor seeking a reward;
> But, as Thyself has loved me, O Everlasting Lord!
> Even so I love Thee, and will love,
> And in Thy Praise will sing;
> Solely because Thou art my God-
> And my Eternal King! [30]

Brands of Christianity that preach doubt as weakness or the devil have manipulated honest questioners for too long. We have to start shouting out that the emperor is naked, instead of allowing ourselves to be silenced by the fearful crowd. Doubt is the grace that allows us to escape from prisons of inadequate belief systems. There is hope for us only if we recognize trends to stifle doubt as abusive and manipulative and refuse to be victimized. The saints of the church knew this. Those who advanced the living faith from strength to greater strength were not unwrinkled party-goers but a sweaty bunch of tearful and often vocally excessive strugglers.

---

[18] Benjamin Jowett, quoted in John P. Bradley, Leo F. Daniels, Thomas C. Jones, compilers, *The International Dictionary of Thoughts* (Chicago: J. G. Ferguson Publishing Company, 1969), 227

[19] Leo Tolstoy, *A Confession and other Religious writings,* Jane Kentish trans. (Harmondsworth, England: Penguin, 1987), 116-17

[20] Paul Tillich, *Systematic Theology, Vol. 1* (Chicago: University of Chicago Press, 1951), 7

[21] Paul Tillich, *A History of Christian Thought* (New York: Simon & Schuster, 1967), 538

[22] Charles Birch, *Regaining Compassion for Humanity and Nature* (St. Louis: Chalice Press, 1993), 180

[23] Thomas S. Kuhn, *The Structure of Scientific Revolutions,* 2nd edn (Chicago: University of Chicago Press 1970).

[24] Birch, *Regaining Compassion,* 60

[25] Frances Ridley Havergal, *The Poems and Hymns of Christ's Sweet Singer,* Tacey Bly ed. (New Canaan, Ct: Keats Publishing, 1977), 5

[26] See my book, Val Webb, *Why We're Equal.*

[27] Benjamin Jowett, Vincent Quinn and John Prest eds., *Dear Miss Nightingale* (Oxford: Oxford University Press, 1987), 4

[28] Bill Stone, *Successful Direct Marketing Methods, 3rd edn.* (Chicago: Crain Books, 1984) 272-3

[29] Professor Leuba, quoted in William James, *The Varieties of Religious Experiences* (New York: Collier Books. 1968), 392.

[30] Author unknown (*O Deus, ego amo te*), translated from Latin to English by Edward Caswell, *Lyra Catholica,* 1849.

Chapter 4.   Tales from the Survivors – Part I

I look upon myself as a child of the age,
a child of unbelief and doubt;
it is probable, nay, I know for certain,
that I shall remain so to my dying day.
I have been tortured with longing to believe –
am so, indeed, even now;
and the yearning grows stronger
the more cogent the intellectual difficulties
that stand in the way.

Fyodor Dostoyevsky (1821-81),[31]

The searchlight that swept wide across the sky in Chapter 2 looked for crusty souls who argued with God, who not always liked the God they found, who questioned unceasingly, not afraid to doubt. The point of that search for saints was to establish that negative attitudes to doubt have not always been the history of Christianity. Chapter 3 traced the development of negativity with regard to doubt and how negativity becomes abusive when authoritative knowledge is used as power over another.

To talk of a theological position as abusive is a serious charge and has something of a shock value. Yet we have discovered in so many instances that any abuse by one person or group of another will continue for as long as the winners or the powerful can name it in positive terms, thus never be challenged. Abusive elements in the colonization of Africa, Australia and South America were rationalized as "for the natives' own good". Women were denied education and freedom in marriage and society because men declared they were ordained to be weak and subordinate "by nature". Children did not report abuse because parents swore them to secrecy under the guise of "loyalty" to the family.

And thousands of people in churches today, and even millions who have left, have suffered lifelong guilt, grief and alienation because those who have claimed authority over them have named the doubting of that authority as sin or weakness. In this chapter, the searchlight will zero in on some who have written about their struggles with abusive attitudes to doubt — some survived to emerge from it and some did not. The pain, the isolation and the despair in the impossibility of their situation rings through their stories. Whereas the earlier chapter featured doubters as ones celebrating the dynamics and health of a "living faith", these biographical vignettes of lives abused because of their doubt, expose the pathological pressures to which they were subjected. By naming negativity to doubt as such, we can move forward to free ourselves from its guilt, embracing and celebrating what doubt really can achieve.

The great hymn writer William Cowper (1731-1800) was plagued by doubt from early in his life. A product of a strict Calvinistic tradition, he was convinced that God would not forgive him. The theological emphasis at that time on the unforgivable sin did nothing to relieve his conviction. At that time, the unforgivable sin was interpreted in two ways:

> (a) the sin of the Pharisees who ascribed Jesus' power to Satan
> (b) a more general sin of consistently denying known truth, or any other form of religious scepticism.

The latter interpretation was a sledge hammer for any form of doubt, a manipulative interpretation to crush the doubter, not just into blaming one's own weakness of faith but rather condemning the doubter irretrievably to damnation. This was combined with the doctrine of predestination that insisted God has already decided from before a person's birth who would be saved and who would be damned.

Cowper's conviction that he was already condemned by his doubts spawned, or at least exacerbated, a series of nervous breakdowns that spanned his life. When the rare moments of sanity and feelings of grace came to him, they were short-lived and he soon felt damned again. "Everything preached to me", he wrote, "and everything preached the curse of the Law". [32] When he was unable to pray, Cowper interpreted this as proof he had sinned against the Holy Spirit. His mentor, slave trader turned Anglican minister John Newton (1725-1807), author of the hymn "Amazing Grace", was confidently certain of his own predestination for salvation and could not understand Cowper's struggle. He wrote to him:

I pity your conflicts and I try not to envy your comforts. You are in safe hands. All your conflicts and all your victories are already marked out for you. [33]

But this was exactly Cowper's concern. His doubts led him to suspect that what was already laid out for him was predestination to damnation and the constant feeling that his soul was "among lions" was evidence of it.

What Cowper needed was a friend who could release him from these doctrines and allow him to address his doubts constructively. Divine nudges *were* present, surfacing as grace in rare moments when he wrote such hymns as "Sometimes a light surprises a Christian while he sings" and "O for a closer walk with God". But for Cowper, the escape to freedom from abuse by a theology which could not countenance doubt did not come in his lifetime. Towards the end, Cowper dreamed that God said, "It is all over with thee. Thou hast perished". Thus he died, believing that God had assigned him to hell.

The great American preacher Harry Emerson Fosdick (1878-1969) knew from childhood that he would embrace religion as his predominant interest and major vocation, yet he soon began to doubt the belief system of his upbringing. In his autobiography, he remembers, as a deeply religious, morbidly conscientious boy, the deplorable effect on him of hell fire teaching, his weeping at night for fear of going to hell and, like Cowper, the agonizing fear of committing the unpardonable sin. His childhood faith received a major blow when he entered college. By second year, nothing would drag Fosdick into a church. He was even labelled a "disturbing upsetter of the saints". Pious souls prayed for his return to the faith, but Fosdick was a long way from returning. The religion that had been the centre of his personal life had been disturbed and he was disturbed from the ground up. While others may pass through this stage of questioning and doubt more easily, Fosdick took it hard. It was a mental rather than moral struggle concerning the intellectual credibility of the Christian faith.

How did Fosdick survive the theological turmoil? He was one of the lucky ones. He finally found a safe space to ask the questions that had not been allowed in his past. He discovered a professor who could "hear" his doubts, not as utterances from someone without faith but as the pain of someone committed to faith who refused to settle for second-hand belief. His mentor showed Fosdick how to be Christian without crucifying his intellect. Fosdick ended his junior year in college "not believing much" but at least believing in the possibility of finding something to believe, that vital difference between faith and beliefs.

Fosdick became convinced that biblical stories did not have to be accepted "as is" simply because they were in the Bible. This understanding gave him access to new ways of thinking, from which he was to reinterpret theology and record his discoveries for others. He was a survivor, able and willing to talk about it and empower others to grow through trusting their own experiences. Fosdick tells of a friend who showed promise as a church leader but who was also turned off by this rigid type of teaching and chastised for his doubts. He became an agnostic, working against the church. Fosdick writes:

> [He] represents a tragedy, repeated innumerable times in my day - a man with the makings of a good Christian, in some of his attitudes and activities, displaying a more Christian spirit than the average run of churchmen, turned into an atheist by the honest necessity of rebelling against a crude, incredible orthodoxy.... Through a lifetime I have watched this endlessly repeated tragedy; defenders of the faith, presenting the faith in indefensible terms, and alienating the minds they might have won. [34]

The father of psychologist Carl Jung (1875-1961) was a pastor in the Swiss Reformed Church. Carl was a religious child who wrestled early in life with doubts about the God in whom his father believed. Like the examples above, he struggled with the unsettling concept of the unforgivable sin but his struggle was different from Fosdick's. Jung somehow felt pressured by God to think thoughts that inevitably would lead to this sin. With considerable emotional turmoil, Jung resisted for months, believing such a surrender would mean damnation. When he could struggle no more, he gave in, exhausted, to this invitation to doubt and experienced a release, a freedom he had not known before.

Jung realized God was not locked in certain doctrines. In fact, Jung believed God had nudged him out of such a prison. God lived omnipotent and free above both Bible and church, calling people to go alone into unknown and perhaps belief-shattering territory. What stopped people, according to Jung, was their desire to deny the existence of any problems, to make their lives simple and smooth, to have certainties not doubts, results without experiments. Any certainties can only arise through doubts and results only through experiment. As a young adult, Jung realized that this freeing moment within himself was something his pastor-father had not experienced and so he hinted as much to his father. The reply was, "Nonsense, you always want to think. One ought not to think, but believe". Jung was appalled that his father could swallow such theories without question:

> Not until several years later did I come to understand that my poor father did not dare to think, because he was consumed by inward doubts. He was taking refuge from himself and therefore insisted on blind faith. He could not receive it as a grace because he wanted to "win it by struggle", forcing it to come with convulsive efforts. [35]

Jung's questions to his father continually met with the same lifeless answers or a resigned shrug. Jung could not see why his father did not grab these opportunities to come to terms with his own religious doubts. All attempts at discussion were finally abandoned and they were alienated by something that could have brought them together, all because his father did not have permission to doubt. On hearing him once in private prayer, Jung realized his father's desperate struggle to keep *any* faith at all and Jung was outraged at the hopeless fortress his father's beliefs had constructed that "blocked all avenues by which [his father] might reach God directly, and then faithlessly abandoned him".[36]

In a similar vein across the ocean, Australian historian Manning Clark (1915-91) watched his Anglican priest father struggle with doubt. He remembers his father telling him as a small child, "Look, boy, I am as sure of [the resurrection] as I am of anything living". [37] Clark never knew, however, whether his father expressed such certainties in order to stifle the doubts that tormented him through his lifetime. In contrast, Clark's mother did not seem worried by doubt:

> My mother could not understand why [my father] needed to "err and stray" from God's ways like a lost sheep. She stood on entrenched ground; my father was never to know the peace of standing on such ground. My mother was never visited by doubts, she never needed to say to herself, "Help thou my unbelief". My father always uttered these words with a fervour which measured the longing in his soul for certainty, anything which would quieten the uproar inside him. [38]

So many people tread such inhospitable territory in their families and groups. Not everyone requires the same rigorous transparency from their belief system. Some who live with the "just believe" mantra cannot understand the person who always struggles for answers. Manning Clark's brother and sister never asked questions, believing what they were told, but Clark "began to doubt everything". He had no one to talk with as his mother dismissed his questions as a bother and warned him that "people will think you're peculiar" having such thoughts. Clark's father always put the discussion off until a "later" that never eventuated — "I got the message that my father did not want to peer into the darkness". [39] This inability of his family circle to face Clark's concerns sent him on a life-long pilgrimage. He wrote, "Whatever the cause, a passionate lover and believer became a doubter, but the doubter never lost his thirst to love or his thirst to believe".[40]

In any field of knowledge and in any era, certain books stand out above all others to become the classics we will read down the years as benchmarks for thought. One such book was Rudolf Otto's (1869-1937) *The Idea of the Holy*, published first in German in 1917. When this book was published, the theological climate was suspicious of piety or any talk of "feelings" or non-rational factors. Otto challenged this with his deliberate inquiry into such non-rational feelings, calling them the sense of the tremendous, the mysterious, the "numinous". As with all such theological challenges, Otto's ideas were formed from his own struggles with doubt. Otto was born into a very religious and strict evangelical Lutheran pietistic home which shaped him early. "I couldn't read any history calmly unless I was convinced beforehand that the people in it were also devout and not 'catholic' or 'Jews' or 'heathens'", Otto wrote.[41] Otto's family argued theological issues with vehemence and Otto longed to get into theological studies, though not in a "too liberal school".

This fear was to be realized, however, when he began studies at Erlangen and was projected forcibly into a personal theological crisis:

> The earth disappeared from under my feet. That was the result of my studies in Erlangen. I went there not so much to quest for truth, but more to vindicate belief. I left with the resolve to seek nothing but the truth, even at the risk of not finding it in Christ. [42]

Research suggests that Otto suffered from deep depression for much of his life and there are unsettled questions as to whether he tried to commit suicide a few times and whether falling to his death from a tower while alone was accidental.   Much of his emotional struggles were closely intertwined with his despair over doubts when his experience did not fit the belief systems. Otto was supported in his despair by his theologian friend Ernst Troelsch (1865-1923) who wrote to him during one of his bouts:

> You must now, above all, pull yourself together, and call to mind the views which you hold for yourself as a man, quite apart from any and every theology. You must have views which are for your own personal use. What you do with theology, we will want to look further into.... If it doesn't go well, then you will just have to begin something quite different. For the moment, attend in general only to peace of mind and the strength of the inner man. [43]

Our searchlight for survivors now swings to England to John Hick (1922-2012), one of the most influential philosophers of religion of the second half of the twentieth century. Hick's writings are also interwoven with personal experience. Having long struggled with doubts when his experience did not fit the theology to which he was exposed, Hick insists that the beginning of faith must be one's own experience of ultimate reality. He also distinguishes between faith and belief. As a child he was taken to an Anglican Sunday service, which he describes as a matter of "infinite boredom". But, he says:

> ....Although the church had nothing directly to do with it, I have from almost as early as I can remember had a rather strong sense of the reality of God as the personal and loving Lord of the universe, and of life as having a meaning within God's purpose. [44]

Hick tells of his teenage search across a variety of religious traditions and of a "spiritual conversion" he underwent in his first year as a Law student in Hull, England. In the company of students of the "evangelical and indeed fundamentalist kind", he was struck by the life and sayings of Jesus and his personality. It was not an easy experience. Hick describes

> ...a period of several days of intense mental and emotional turmoil during which I was powerfully aware of a higher truth and greater reality pressing in upon my consciousness and claiming my recognition and response. At first this intrusion was highly unwelcome, a disturbing and challenging

demand for nothing less than a revolution in personal identity.   But presently the disturbing claim became a liberating invitation and I entered with great joy into the world of Christian faith. [45]

Hick accepted as a whole and without question what he calls "the entire evangelical package of theology" - verbal inspiration of the Bible, creation and a fall, Jesus as God the Son incarnate, born of a virgin, conscious of his divine nature, performing miracles of divine power, redemption by his blood from sin and guilt, his bodily resurrection and ascension and future return in glory, heaven and hell. His plan to enter the Christian ministry was interrupted by the Second World War, during which he joined the Friends' Ambulance Unit. Yet already he was struggling with "a certain narrowness and a lack of sympathy with questioning thought" within his Christian circle.

As Hick began to doubt some of the theological positions of his group, he experienced from his peers something in which he had previously taken part — resentment towards those who raised awkward questions that upset established orthodoxy.   Hick sees it as inevitable that those with a questioning mind will eventually have to face their doubts when the vision of one's belief system becomes too small. Hick carefully separates out what is happening here.

> The response to Jesus Christ as one's Lord, and as one's Saviour from alienation from God, may be the same; but the body of theological theories associated with it in one's mind will usually change, and surely ought to change, in the light of further living, learning, and thinking. [46]

I quote at length Hick's description of his "conversion" and the dramatic experience of faith as a relationship with something ultimate that stemmed from that conversion, even though subsequently the belief systems crumbled around him. Part of the tactics of those who use doubt as a negative against those who question is to suggest that doubt is the result of an inadequate, false or failed conversion attempt, something that "didn't take properly". Thus questioning becomes the fault of the questioner, not the theories offered. Hick goes on to talk of specific challenges to his beliefs — the question of suffering and evil given the reality of a loving God; the question of truth in other religions emerging from his multicultural experiences in Birmingham, England; and the question of the interpretation of the incarnation of Jesus as "divine Son of God".

For Hick, following his doubts was not easy because of the alienation and opposition he experienced. Yet, it was the move that was "historically honest" for him. In this, he speaks for many, many doubters when he describes the loss in moving beyond old traditions with their mystery and magic that aroused emotive warm feelings of religious certainty. However, while many church members are content with such traditions and resist change, others simply cannot. Hick says of these people, including himself:

> Thus we have to live in tension which is painful, and can only be avoided by either cutting oneself off from the church and its old liturgy and imagery, or refuse to listen to the voices of rationality or the conviction of a divine presence transcending our own particular mythology. [47]

This "tension" Hick describes, however painful at times when one is tempted to smother one's doubts and go with the flow of blind belief, is a creative tension that draws us beyond passive acceptance and launches us into new worlds of thought and experience. For Hick, this did not lead to the loss of "faith" but rather to a whole new awareness of ultimate reality across many religious traditions, something he claimed to be an inbuilt human capacity. How many millions of people do we need, he asks, who have claimed an experience of Presence across the centuries describing it in their own culturally conditioned religious ways, before we take notice:

> The Real, or the Transcendent — whose nature is transcategorical, beyond the scope of our human concepts — is that which must be if human religious experience globally is not delusion. We cannot know it as it is in itself, but we know it as it affects us. [48]

American theologian John Cobb (1925-) has dedicated his long and influential career to interpreting the thinking of the English philosopher Alfred North Whitehead (1861-1947) whose "process thought" has been useful for theology today. Cobb grew up with his missionary parents in Japan. He recalls that, as far back as he can remember, he was conscious of himself as a Christian, not just because his family was but in the subjective sense that he had internalized the desire to be a Christian "so intensely that I sometimes found my parents' more relaxed and balanced attitudes offensive".[49] Those of you who have experienced the intensity of religious devotion as a child will smile in empathetic recognition at this description. Cobb says he was more self-consciously Christian than most of the Christians around him, feeling an urgent and peculiar responsibility to witness to all who talked to him — "looking and acting pious in the objectionable sense" are his words. This burden did not fit well with ordinary childhood experiences, producing in him a confusion of piety and rebellion.

> I was often uncomfortable doing things that would have been perfectly wholesome and, on the hand, at times my natural youthful needs broke through my controls in unattractive and unhealthy ways. There are real problems being too devout too young. [50]

Cobb describes joining every religion organization in his teenage years, organizing prayer groups, covenanting with friends to live strictly disciplined lives and sending his little allowance to lepers in the Sudan. At the same time, however, other religious and ethical ideas were challenging him and presenting him with a disconcerting experience of an open and exploratory Christianity rather than his exclusive, reactionary brand. Cobb decided to be a minister and entered the University of Chicago Humanities School where he discovered that his southern Methodist piety was only one, quite peculiar form of religious life and, in fact, Christianity in *any* form was highly questionable:

> In a few months, I discovered that my understanding of Christianity melted away through my exposure to the thought of the modern world. I was appalled at how quickly a faith I had thought so secure was undercut. I experienced what we have since come to call "the death of God", and it felt very much like my own spiritual death as well. [51]

Cobb calls these events terrifying, but he decided to face his doubts head-on rather than spend the next three years "hammering nails into the coffin of my childhood God". He transferred to the University of Chicago Divinity School to investigate contemporary alternatives to his childhood theology. He was one of the fortunate doubters. Not only was he able to recognize the theological prison into which he had been locked but he immediately encountered a philosopher theologian in Charles Hartshorne (1897-2000) who introduced him to Process theology where a God shape could gradually come alive for him again. Looking back, Cobb recognizes that, had he encountered any other brand of defence of God at that critical time in his thinking, it would not have checked his "drift into atheistic modernity".

> At that time I could not respond to the dogmatic theology of Barth or the
> kerygmatic theology of Bultmann.   Neither Tillich nor neo-Thomism
> spoke convincingly to my doubts...The brilliant analyses of human nature
> and destiny by Reinhold Niebuhr had already moved and grasped me, but
> they did not deal directly with my experience of the disappearance of
> God.... Even now, looking back, it seems that my taking the Hartshornian-
> Whiteheadian direction was not the mere consequence of the chance
> encounter with Hartshorne.   It seems more to be the one possibility of
> belief that was open to me in the intellectual world of the late forties. [52]

Today's Progressive Christianity movement, also known as emerging
Christianity (about which we will talk later) seems to have doubt as its
prerequisite. One of its most popular authors, Marcus Borg (1942-), tells of
growing up in North Dakota in a Scandinavian Lutheran family. Church
was the centre of their lives. In his early teens, Borg's doubts about God's
existence began, filling him with anxiety, guilt and fear of going to hell.
Every night for several years he prayed, "Lord, I believe. Help thou my
unbelief", but his inability to overcome doubt confirmed that he was
becoming more of an unbeliever than a believer. He writes:

> In retrospect, I can also see that, for me at least, belief is not a matter of the
> will. I desperately wanted to believe and to be delivered from the anguish I
> was experiencing. If I could have made myself believe, I would have.[53]

In college, Borg's nightly prayers for belief stopped — "Apparently I no
longer believed enough to be frightened of hell", he says. Fortunately Borg,
like Cobb, encountered in a required religion course in his junior year a
brilliant young professor, Paul Sponheim (1930-), whose course covered all
the big questions and allowed "the sacred cows of inherited belief ... to fall in
a way that legitimated their demise".[54] (This is music to my ears as I
encountered this same brilliant and caring professor in my doctoral studies
and his lectures on Process theology gave me new and authentic theological
language to embrace). In Borg's mid-thirties, he had a number of mystical
experiences — "moments of connectedness in which I felt my linkage to
what is".   These enabled him to re-imagine God, not as something
supernatural out there, but as the "sacred centre of existence, the holy
mystery that is all around us and within us". God was no longer some
doctrinal structure to be believed but was "an element of experience". [55]

Bishop John Shelby Spong has changed the religious landscape forever
with his best seller books challenging so much of traditional Christian

thought. As he point outs in his preface to *Why Christianity must Change or Die: A Bishop speaks to believers in exile,* "I can hardly be mentioned in the public press without the adjective *controversial* being attached to my name. That word has almost become a part of my identity".[56] Growing up in the American Deep South, Spong as a young boy was initiated into racism, homophobia and the subordination of women as the unquestioned way of life. As he grew up and studied, doubts about each of these "Christian" positions arose in his mind. Taking seriously the motto of the seminary in which he was trained, "Seek the truth come whence it may, cost what it will", Spong has been at the forefront of calling the Christian church to accountability in its attitude to gay lesbian transgender and bisexual people, to women's status and to racism. In also confronting, with his own considerable scholarship, the bondage caused by fundamentalism and a literal reading of scripture, his writings have freed so many who remain in the church or who have left it as church alumni. He writes:

> Institutional Christianity seems fearful of inquiry, fearful of freedom, fearful of knowledge - indeed, fearful of anything except its own repetitious propaganda, which has its origins in a world that none of us any longer inhabits. The Church historically has been willing to criticize, marginalize, or even expel its most creative thinkers. [57]

There are common threads in the stories thus far. Many had theological training or, in the case of Jung, had allowed theology to impact their intellectual disciplines. While there are millions of doubters that could have been selected who have not had theological education, there is method in my selection because one of the weapons used against the doubter is that doubt comes from a lack of both faith *and* knowledge. Authorities held up as purveyors of "true" doctrine usually claim their power from their superior training in the theological intricacies of the debate. Yet here, a parade of great thinkers demonstrates their common experience of being early victims to the control of thought (and thus the negation of doubt) through the possession by others of "correct knowledge".

Another common thread is that they all speak of the experience of some sort of ultimate reality as crucial to their search, even through dark periods of doubt. No matter how tenuous belief systems became, something or someone seemed to grasp them and hold them, sometimes just barely above water-line. Something within them refused to condemn their doubts as failure and sin, but watered and nurtured their doubts until they were strong and ornery enough to break out of their dark, moist soil into a sunlight where they could stretch and blossom freely. Even in Cowper's sad life, he was aware of God at work, even though his belief system refused to let him see it as positive action. Those who merchandise a religiosity that measures a prescribed "spiritual experience" against doubt as proof of salvation have never met the God that suffers with, that supports the drooping head, that "sighs too deeply for words".

---

[31] Fyodor Dostoyevsky, *The Brothers Karamazov*, quoted in Karen Armstrong, *A History of God: the 4000 year quest of Judaism, Christianity and Islam* (New York: Alfred A. Knopf, 1993) 359

[32] Maurice J. Quinlan, *William Cowper: a Critical Life* (Minneapolis: University of Minnesota Press, 1935), 36-7.

[33] Quinlan, *William Cowper*, 86.

[34] Harry Emerson Fosdick, *The Living of These Days: an autobiography* (New York: Harper & Brothers, 1956), 21-2.

[35] C. G. Jung, *Memories, Dreams, Reflections,* Aniela Jaffe ed., (New York: Pantheon Books. 1961), 73

[36] Jung, *Memories*, 93

[37] Manning Clark, *The Puzzles of Childhood: his early life* (Ringwood, Victoria: Penguin, 1989), 7

[38] Clark, *The Puzzles of Childhood*, 38

[39] Clark, *The Puzzles of Childhood*, 95

[40] Clark, *The Puzzles of Childhood*, 74

[41] Rudolf Otto, quoted in Philip C. Almond, *Rudolf Otto: an introduction to his philosophical theology* (Chapel Hill & London: The University of North Carolina Press, 1984), 10.

[42] Almond, *Rudolf Otto*, 12

[43] Almond, *Rudolf Otto*, 16

[44] John Hick, *God has Many Names* (Philadelphia: The Westminster Press, 1980), 14

[45] Hick, *God has Many Names*, 14

[46] Hick, *God has Many Names*, 16

[47] John Hick, *The Problem of Religious Pluralism* (New York: St. Martin's Press, 1985), 16

[48] John Hick, *The New Frontier of Religion and Science: religious experience, neuroscience and the transcendent* (Hampshire: Palgrave Macmillan, 2006), 206

[49] John B. Cobb, Jr., *Can Christ become Good News Again?* (St. Louis: Chalice Press, 1991), 3

[50] Cobb, *Can Christ become good news again?*, 3

[51] Cobb, *Can Christ become good news again?*, 8

[52] David Tracy & John B. Cobb, Jr., *Talking about God: doing theology in the context of modern pluralism* (New York: Seabury Press, 1983), 41-2

[53] Marcus Borg, *Meeting Jesus again for the First Time* (New York: HarperSanFrancisco, 1994), 7.

[54] Marcus Borg, *Meeting Jesus again*, 8

[55] Marcus Borg, *Meeting Jesus again*, 14-5

[56] John Shelby Spong, *Why Christianity must Change or Die: a bishop speaks to believers in exile* (New York: HarperSanFranciso,1998), ix

[57] Spong, *Why Christianity must Change or Die*, 4-5

Chapter 5.   Tales from the Survivors – Part II

For as long as I can remember, God and I have not been able to leave
each other alone. I have searched with all my heart for God and have
often not liked the God I found. I have bent myself in "sweet
surrender" and have angrily challenged. I have felt pursued by the
"Hound of Heaven" and have struggled in the grip of a [G]od who
deserves to be rejected. Through it all, one thing has become clear. I
am so constructed - genes? early experiences? temperamental
inclination? - that the search will not, cannot be abandoned. Images of
God may be found and rejected, replaced and revamped, sometimes
absolutely lacking - but the search goes on.

Mary Jo Meadow [58]

Observant readers will have noticed another common thread in the examples of the previous chapter — and I hope you have not put down the book in disgust as a result! All the examples of doubters were *men*. I have grouped them this way on purpose because I want to discuss another element in the tyranny of doubt as personal failure. It is not that men doubt differently from women. However, if negative attitudes to doubt have been perpetuated by theological arguments, we must reflect on the fact that, until the last fifty years or so, theology has been almost exclusively in the hands of *men* and any conclusions arrived at come from *men's* experience of the world. Not many of them questioned whether it was appropriate for men to incorporate their view of the world into theological conclusions and then simply generalize to include women.

This is not the place for a full discussion of feminist theology, something I have already mentioned. However, the same theological arguments that have named doubt as a negative have also named women as subordinate to men because of the natural rules of creation. This argument was developed from a literal reading of the Genesis creation story - women were "helpmates" created secondarily "out of man" and Eve was responsible for Adam eating the apple, causing God to give men the rule over women. All this was bolstered by various references in later New Testament letters to women being silent in church and subordinate to husbands at home. If these passages are read literally, such conclusions may be reached, but such a reading ignores any consideration of the context from which the text emerged, how women were viewed culturally at the time in relation to men, or how the text may have been used politically in the social context of the day. Women who have believed their doubts are evidence of inadequacy experience a *double* whammy of self-flagellating doubt. Not only are they inferior and less spiritual as doubters, they are also inferior and less spiritual as women.

Valerie Saiving (1921-92) first broke the silence about this problem. Sin has traditionally been defined as pride in Christianity, the defiant attempt of the human to be like God, to take the place of God. Certainly in a culture where the male is head of the household, the voting member of the family, the unquestioned authority in all matters, as men were in the centuries when traditional theologies were formulated, sin against God could well be described as pride in seeking to be God for oneself. But in that same period, women had no power, no vote and no authority and were punished for challenging the authority of their male head, let alone God. How then could their sin be "pride" which led them to try to substitute themselves for God when they could not even breach the authority of their own husbands?

Despite this, women as well as men in one generic sweep were constantly entreated in sermons and books to espouse humility, denial of self and self sacrifice, solutions for the sin of pride. While such entreaties urged men to relinquish a little of their arrogant independence before God, the same plea suggested women move into *more* self-negation and denial of self than they already exhibited. To be a good Christian woman meant more self-effacing behaviour, more submission and thus openness to domination and abuse. For women, to turn the other cheek was not a noble refusal to avenge affronted male pride but rather to endure the physical or emotional abuse of a violent husband for the seventh time that week. Perhaps, Saiving suggests, women's "sin" is not their pride but their *lack* of it – lack of respect for their own selfhood as created in God's image.

In the same way, "virtue" in men refers to qualities of exemplary leadership, nobility, bravery, steadfastness, manliness and other public qualities of male greatness. The word comes from the Latin *vir* meaning "man" and, in ancient Rome, was first linked to military courage and bravery but, in time, was applied more broadly to men who did the right thing in society. The word was not used for women in Roman society — their superior quality was *pudicitia* meaning "modesty" or "chastity", from the word *pudor* or the shame of not behaving properly in society. To speak of "virtuous women" is not to expect that they be fair leaders, brave public role models or noble heroes. Rather, the virtuous woman must possess characteristics that men would see as *weakness* in the male - submissive, quiet, long-suffering, faithful in morals and meek. Thus, when we are encouraged to virtue in the scriptures and in the church, it has very different meanings for men and women.

In the same way, the gifts of the Spirit — love, joy, peace, long-suffering, gentleness, patience, meekness, self-control — are quoted so glibly by those who moralize about the Christian life but, if taken one by one, they are lived out and valued differently for men and women. Saiving's doubts as a *woman* about theology took many years to compost and she began her famous essay of 1960 that jump-started feminist theology with the words:

> I am a student of theology; I am also a woman. Perhaps it strikes you as curious that I put these two assertions beside each other, as if to imply that one's sexual identity has some bearing on his theological views. I myself would have rejected such an idea when I first began my theological studies. But now, thirteen years later, I am no longer so certain as I once was that, when theologians speak of 'man', they are using the word in its generic sense. It is, after all, a well-known fact that theology has been written almost exclusively by men. This alone should put us on guard, especially since contemporary theologians constantly remind us that one of man's strongest temptations is to identify his own limited perspective with universal truth. [59]

This is why I have separated women's experience of doubt from that of men because women's doubts arise, not only from the discrepancy between their experiences and prevalent belief systems, as do men's, but also because of the discrepancy between male and female experiences in a gendered society. This is more than a biological issue. Societies designate different *roles* and behavioural norms for men and women which must be taken into consideration before simply describing human experience and theological norms in a generic male-based way.

When I first read the writings of the feminist theologians of the seventies, my spirit instantly bonded and reverberated with what they were saying because I had experienced those same doubts myself about the so-called roles of Christian women and now knew that it was not my problem alone. However, when my daughter read these same women theologians in the nineties in her more gender-balanced university climate, she was less impressed as she had no concept of the exhilaration of those early days of women's discoveries and little comprehension of how women could have allowed themselves to be so dominated and silenced, negating their own experiences. Yet this is the evil of any abuse, the unquestioned assumption that doubts about a situation that does not fit one's experience are simply one's own problem. Only those who have been "heard to speech" out of silence can understand.

Mary Jo Meadow (1936-) is a retired American professor of psychology and religious studies, a Catholic sister, a teacher of insight meditation in the Theravada Buddhist tradition and a mother of eight. Her current interests focus on integrating Buddhist meditation practice with the Christian contemplative prayer tradition. Yet her autobiographical writings tell of her childhood struggle with doubts, generated both by her gender and her experiences within an oppressive theology. She was an intensely religious child, encouraged by Catholic parents of a dogmatic, legalistic and miracle-seeking generation. As a seven year old, she avidly read biographies of women saints, no doubt chosen as role models for her, and was captivated by "an elusive goal of goodness and God-givenness" which she tried to imitate:

> I read a biography of St. Rose of Lima. Her willing endurance of suffering - even her seeking out ways to prefer herself least - greatly impress me. For weeks, I follow her practice of trying to choose the most stale pieces of bread for oneself. [60]

At nine, Meadow faced an experience no doubt shared by many young girls growing up in her era, something that sent her into the agony of fear that her actions would put her beyond God's reach.

> I am curious about my body and explore "down there" to see what it is like. I know that I have done something horribly wrong! But how can I tell the priest, who is a man, about this? In the confessional, I tell him that I was "nasty". He asks me what I mean. I can only repeat that I was just nasty. He asks, "You mean like unkind to your friends?" Relieved to have some way out of the situation, I mutter, "Yes" - and live for some time in

fear that I have dammed myself to hell, even long after I could rationally argue against this conclusion. [61]

The struggles of her teen years are painful to read, an intellectual mind in collision with her parent's literal faith that did not work for her. When she tried to raise the issues with her parents or a nun who visited the family, there was no attempt to deal honestly with her questions, many which have now been publicly addressed by the Catholic Church. Instead, she was told that her doubt was damming her to hell and the only answer was to value, as she ought, the "gift of faith" available to her through the church. The irony was that Meadow did not want to walk away from God but towards God. She yearned for the way, but came close to despairing of finding what she sought. She told her parents that she was not interested in God if God was how *they* saw God, waiting to pounce when we try to be honest with ourselves. She was told that we cannot decide how God is, but learn to love God as God is. Meadow spent hours in her bedroom pleading:

> God, I do want to belong to you, but I am just so confused and I don't know how. I don't mind paying what it costs - I am willing to suffer with God, but things just don't feel right. And I don't know what to do or where to go or who to talk to. [62]

After graduation from a Jesuit college, marriage, three children in three years and one brain-damaged, Meadow continued not using birth control, regularly attended church and accepted the blows she had been dealt with stoic grace — until the day she found she could no longer believe. Naturally, she blamed herself.

> My faith in God, my trust of God was not deep enough. I was not truly given to God.... Briefly I dared to get angry with God: "If you're up there, at least make it possible for me to believe in you, since I need you so much". But I backed off quickly, and asked again what flaw in myself made me unable to believe as others did, filled me with doubts and questions.... The hell I was in became deeper and deeper. [63]

Meadow's solution was to throw herself into "finding faith" again, teaching Sunday School, trying to pray, having another child, yet having no one to speak to about her pain. Her story does not end here, but at this point she was the epitome of a victim of theological abuse. Her experience within herself drew her to God unceasingly, if not often angrily because of God's opaqueness, yet there was no one on her horizon who could release her from the box into which her doctrines had locked her.

Meadow's Catholic upbringing contributed to her inability to question because of the authority given to church teachings. Lest Protestant sisters see her experience as unique to Catholicism, this continues in Protestant traditions using the scriptures as a weapon. Catholic theologian Rosemary Radford Ruether, a contemporary of Meadow, who has brilliantly challenged her church on its oppressive and sexist attitude to women, did not grow up with the literal interpretations of scripture with which her Protestant sisters have had to contend. In her Catholic theological upbringing, she studied the sacraments endlessly but never opened a Bible. Thus she first came to the Bible with all the modern apparatus of historical-critical thought and little of the baggage that comes from literal readings of the text, which she calls a debilitating obstacle to spiritual freedom. Observing the pain in her sisters subjected to such authoritative approaches, she feels less betrayed by the biblical world because she happened upon it with a more realistic approach to what it is.

> I never assumed that [the Bible] dropped out of heaven undefiled by historical gestation. Rather, I understand it as a product of a human quest for meaning that moved through many different stages and contexts. It is certainly not all of a piece, and it is incomprehensible to me why anyone would expect it to be. It is shaped by, dependent on, and yet responding to, the religious world around it. [64]

For retired religion professor Rita Gross (1943-), another contemporary of Meadow and Ruether, the inability of the religious tradition into which she was born to address her doubts eventually led her out of the church and into Judaism, then Buddhism. Gross, a young girl seeking intellectual and spiritual adventure, grew up in a small log cabin on a humble dairy farm in northern Wisconsin. While her mother wanted her to settle back on a farm, Gross saw religion as the arena where life's questions were asked and answered. She was, however, confined in the dogmatic and narrow Wisconsin Synod of the Lutheran Church which could not abide her questioning, especially about their version of the doctrine of "no salvation outside the church". In college, Gross was reprimanded for participating in the "wrong kind" of Lutheran Church choir and responded that she believed *all* religions were striving for the same goal but using different methods. She was told her opinion was erroneous and heretical and, at her mother's funeral, was targeted through an anti-Semitic and anti-intellectual sermon (she was studying Hebrew language and civilization at the time). A few months later, she was excommunicated for heresy and consigned to hell in church opinion. While this was traumatic, Gross says that the deepest trauma of her religious life was still to come when she began to realize the enormity of the subordination of women in Christianity, linked to the gendering of God as male. The repressed anger she had felt from childhood at being a woman was not, as she had thought, about being *female*, but rather at the treatment meted out to women — limitations, discrimination and stereotyping all sanctioned by God within the church. [65]

Meadow, Gross and Ruether all come from the beginnings of the feminist theology movement of the sixties and seventies. There are many stories of such women finding their voices and getting angry over injustices done to women by enforcing their silence. By talking together, women began to see patterns in shared experiences and found strength in shouting unladylike in the streets for recognition and justice. No longer need they squelch their hidden doubts about the "rules" for women as some fault within themselves. Women began to name their liberating God in metaphors from their own experiences as women, rather than living vicariously through descriptions from men's experiences, like Aesop's fable of the lion and the statue.

> A man and a lion were discussing the relative strengths of men and lions in general. The man contended that he and his fellows were stronger than lions by reason of their greater intelligence. "Come now with me", he cried, "and I will soon prove that I am right". So he took him into the public gardens and showed him a statue of Hercules overcoming the lion and tearing his mouth in two. "That's all very well", said the lion, "but proves nothing, for it was a man who made the statue". [66]

The first draft of this book was written in "white heat" in the summer of 1989 before I became immersed in my Ph. D. in theology and before I had been exposed to feminist theology in a serious way. It was the product of my own long struggle with doubt in a theological tradition that blamed the doubter and had little sympathy with questions that challenged basic belief structures. In my own way, I had come to the conclusion that my doubts would always surface if suppressed and that it was time I accepted them for the creative nudges they really were and learn to celebrate them.

This watershed in my journey forced me to write down the manipulation to which my doubts had always been subjected. I submitted the book to a publisher and the editor contacted me to tell me he might be interested, but that there was a glaring problem. I was a women writer and yet almost all the examples in my book were of men. While we both were aware that this was due in part to the lack of women writing in theology during Christian history, he gently chided me that I had not sought out experiences of women to include.

As I moved further into feminist theology, I put on hold the re-writing of the book because I was making a tremendous discovery. I too was experiencing the "yeah-yeah" reaction as I listened to my once-silenced sisters. I was discovering that my autobiography was not just a story of a *doubter*, but it was the story of a *woman* who was a doubter. I was beginning to see that many of the issues I had questioned from my early days were not only about dogmatic theology but also about a theology which was abusive to women's wholeness and equality. I became aware of the insidiousness of negativity towards doubt from another perspective — that of a woman.

I grew up in the tradition described by many of the serious doubters I have introduced here. I learned early that to be "saved", one must make a personal and public commitment to Jesus Christ and that personal assurance of this salvation would follow as proof of the efficacy of the act. Such feelings of assurance would sweep away all doubt. Because this act of commitment required a certain prescriptive repetition of words inviting Jesus into the heart, there was always the chance, if the subsequent spiritual feeling did not stay permanently, that the words had not been said correctly or had not "taken". This caused anxiety and led to continual re-dedication "just in case", since responsibility for gaining eternal life seemed to lie heavily on one's own action and intention in inviting God into the heart. Many times in my adolescent life I was overwhelmed with panic when I heard an invitation to commit one's life to Christ. Even though I had said the "required words" hundreds of times, I was always afraid my doubts might have invalidated them and thus, if I refused the current appeal, I may have lost my chance for eternity — inadvertently screwed up.

Doubts about the state of my soul played havoc. Did I feel any different? No. Then perhaps I didn't say the right words? But I did. Then perhaps I was not sincere in my heart and God knew and did not accept them? Perhaps...perhaps... Doubts bred doubts all over again while I felt totally condemned by the very fact that I was doubting. These doubts were fed to unhealthy size by the confidence and assurance exuding from others around me who demonstrated, by conversation liberally infused with phrases of "what the Lord has done for me", their total absence of doubt. Many of these people, I have to report, have left Christianity altogether in their mature years.

Growing up Born Again is a delightful tongue-in-cheek book written by a group of adults who grew up in a tradition with the constant pressure to be assured of salvation, to be free of doubt and the resulting insidious cycle of guilt and inward turmoil about doubt.

> Revival meetings...are held for two purposes: to get sinners saved from the fire of hell and to get Christians fired up. On any given night you may walk into the church feeling sure that you're a Christian. But by the time the sermon is over you're not so sure. After four verses of "Oh, Why Not Tonight?" you're quite certain that you've been living a lie. You know you should go forward, but you don't want to. It's pride, you realize. You shouldn't let pride stand between you and the Lord.

The decisive punch in the appeal was always along the line of the man who hesitated and was killed by a train on the way home.

> The evangelist's wife plays the song through one more time and yes, you go forward. You don't want there to be any mistake in God's mind. When you're hit by a train, your name will be written in the Book of Life. [67]

One of the most dramatic confessions of doubt in recent years comes from the letters of Mother Teresa (1910-97), that icon of compassion who first springs to everyone's mind as an example of selfless faith and devotion. Her letters to her confessor and other mentors were published in 2007, ten years after her death, and tell of years and years of darkness and doubt in her soul, even as she was accomplishing so much for the utterly poor and destitute of Calcutta. As a child and a young Loreto nun, she had experienced a close union with God which her confessor describes as being "inundated with light":

> The Voice that she had heard spoke to her tender words of love, flooding her soul with consolations, and the closer she drew to Him, the more she longed her Him. [68]

Such conviction of God led her to step out and found the Missionaries of Charities to work with the poor. At this point, darkness enclosed her and she was unable to feel God's presence. She wrote:

> ...this terrible sense of loss — this untold darkness — this loneliness — this continual longing for God — which gives me such pain deep down in my heart. —Darkness is such that I really do not see — neither with my mind nor with my reason. — The place of God in my soul is blank. — There is no God for me. — When the pain of longing is so great — I just long and long for God — and then it is that I feel — He does not want me — He is not there. [69]

This was not some fleeting experience but continued through her life work. At a spiritual retreat in 1985, she told her confessor of this excruciating night of the soul, saying:

> Father, I do realize that when I open my mouth to speak to the sisters and to people of God about God's work, it brings them light, joy and courage. But I get nothing of it. Inside it is all dark and feeling that I am totally cut off from God". [70]

To cope with this reality, Mother Teresa named her mission as being a "saint of darkness", continually absent from heaven to light the light of those in darkness on earth.

While Mother Teresa rationalized her doubts and stayed a nun, religion scholar Karen Armstrong (1944-) entered the convent in 1962 at seventeen and would eventually leave, "having suffered a mild breakdown, obscurely broken and damaged".[71] The convent's loss was the world's gain as Armstrong then applied her brilliant mind, so belittled in the convent, to wrestle with the great questions of religion for the benefit of us all. Armstrong's motivation for entering the convent was to find God:

> God would no longer be a remote, shadowy reality but a vibrant presence in my life. I would see him wherever I looked, and I myself would be transfigured ... I would be serene, joyful, inspired and inspiring. [72]

Despite her striving to be the best nun she could, to count the world but loss for God, God seemed to disappear, leaving a curious blank and an inability to pray.

Our whole existence had God as its pivot. The silence of our days had
been designed to enable us to listen to him. But he had never spoken to
me ... Every morning I resolved that this time I would crack it. This time
there would be no distractions. I would kneel as intent upon God as my
sisters, none of whom seemed to have any difficulties. I had never before
had any problems of concentration. I had always been able to immerse
myself in my studies for hours at a time. But to my intense distress, I
found that I could not keep my mind on God for two minutes. [73]

Armstrong hugged this "shameful secret" for seven years, having been told
that, without prayer, her religious life was a sham — "This disgrace festered
corrosively at the very heart of my life and spilled over into everything,
poisoning each activity".[74] But it was not only her inability to pray:

The young nuns were constantly told "incredible and irrational" things
that only seemed thus "because we were lacking in spiritual maturity". So
when we were tempted to question the ideas, principles and customs of the
order, we must remember that as yet we were simply not in a position to
understand. We were like babies, learning an entirely new language. One
day, in the not too distant future, when we had developed spiritually, we
would see all these matters quite differently. Until then, we just had to
wait patiently, in what the mystics had called the cloud of unknowing, and
all would be revealed. [75]

The Mother Superior, standing in the place of God, was always right — "It
was simply my wretched intellectual pride that blocked my spiritual
advancement, and I would make no progress as long as I refused to regard
things from a supernatural point of view".[76] When Armstrong confessed to
her superiors that she had never had an encounter with anything
supernatural, they thought she was being wayward:

So even in the convent, God had been conspicuous by his absence from my
life. And that, I became convinced, must be my fault. My case seemed so
peculiar that it could not be a mere failure of the system. If only I had tried
a little harder, concentrated just that little bit more, or found more
interesting topics for meditation. [77]

These stories of struggle with creative doubts not able to be expressed
are unfortunately still the pattern in many communities of the faithful.
Doubts are sins and weaknesses, termites in the foundations rather than
wings to fly. What doubters need is for someone to recognize their isolated

captivity and give them permission to take the first step out of it. Doubts are part of an ongoing process of faith but the first step is key - to accept that doubts are not negative but positive. The question church communities need to ask of themselves is "How do we provide a space of safety where people can voice their struggles in public and not be banished back into silence because of their doubts?" Even those churches who acknowledge in theory that there may be different ways to come to God have not provided, in practice, safe spaces to come out of the closet of doubts and share honest discussion.

---

[58] Mary Jo Meadow & Carole A. Rayburn eds., *A Time to Weep, a Time to Sing: faith journeys of women scholars of religion* (Minneapolis: Winston Press Inc., 1985), 233

[59] Valerie Saiving, "The Human Situation: a Feminine View", in Carol P. Christ & Judith Plaskow, eds., *Womenspirit Rising: a feminist reader in religion* (New York: Harper & Row, 1979), 25

[60] Meadow & Rayburn, *A Time to Weep*, 234

[61] Meadow & Rayburn, *A Time to Weep*, 234-5.

[62] Meadow & Rayburn, *A Time to Weep*, 237

[63] Meadow & Rayburn, *A Time to Weep*, 239

[64] Rosemary Radford Ruether, *Disputed Questions: on being a Christian*. (Maryknoll: Orbis Books, 1989), 31

[65] Meadow & Rayburn, *A Time to Weep*, 32-8.

[66] *Aesop's Fables*, quoted in David M. Gunn & Danna Nolan Fewell, *Narrative in the Hebrew Bible* (Oxford: Oxford University Press, 1993), 189

[67] Patricia Klein, Evelyn Bence, Jane Campbell, Laura Pearson & David Wimbish, *Growing Up Born Again,* (New Jersey: Fleming H. Revell Co. Publishers, 1987), 123

[68] Mother Teresa, *Come be My Light: the private writings of the "Saint of Calcutta"*, Brian Kolodiejchuk, M. C. ed. (New York: Doubleday, 2007), 335

[69] Mother Teresa, *Come be My Light*, 1-2

[70] Mother Teresa, *Come be my Light*, 306

[71] Karen Armstrong, *The Spiral Staircase: a memoir* (London: Harper Perennial, 2004), 6

[72] Armstrong, *The Spiral Staircase*, 2

[73] Armstrong, *The Spiral Staircase*, 58-9

[74] Armstrong, *The Spiral Staircase*, 60

[75] Armstrong, *The Spiral Staircase*, 52

[76] Armstrong, *The Spiral Staircase*, 54

[77] Armstrong, *The Spiral Staircase*, 63

Chapter 6.   The Mechanics of Healthy Doubt

Theology is like a garment we have produced, not a universal truth.
The garment, like all garments, will fit some, and not fit others.
Should garments be thrown out then, because they do not fit everyone?
Ah, then we should freeze in the winters of our loneliness! Better we
should simply adjust the fit and see to helping others as they, too,
weave their mantels.

Marjorie Suchocki (1933-) [78]

Frederick Buechner offers "soothing oil" for those who find themselves escaping battered and bruised from negative attitudes toward doubt. For him doubts are part of the religious journey and the range of doubts is as wide as the variety of people.

> I have never assumed that the people I talk to are so certain [God] is true that the question is not still very much alive for them. Is anyone ever that certain? I assume always that even the most religiously disillusioned and negative among them want it to be true as much as the relatively devout do - want to be shown it, want it to be made somehow flesh before their eyes, want to be able to rejoice in it for themselves. [79]

The issue of whether God is true is not the only doubt that arises in religious belief. Challenges to traditions come in many forms. There are challenges to meaning - the meaning of God, the meaning and purpose of the world and of our own purpose. There are challenges to the accumulated traditions of our belief system, arising from discrepancies between beliefs and experiences. And there are challenges to the superiority of one religion or the need for any religion at all.

These challenges, both to the claims of religion and also the interpretations of these claims, come from changes in our world, our culture, our knowledge and our experience. None of us exists outside our culture. Events of history, advances in science, psychology, philosophy, language and communication all influence our thinking. Although each of us develops images of how we want life, the world and God to be for us, our experience is not always like the picture we draw. And what we call God has the habit of acting in ways not prescribed by us. We constantly have to rewrite our schedule, expand the plot of the play.

According to psychiatrist author Scott M. Peck (1936-2005), as such changes reveal more possibilities, our life maps become larger and more accurate. Yet many simply quit their map drawing at twenty and many more at fifty, feeling their maps are correct, even sacrosanct:

> Only a relative and fortunate few continue until the moment of death exploring the mystery of reality, ever enlarging and refining and redefining their understanding of the world and what is true. [80]

With encouragement from such as Buechner and Peck, we will now move from the negative images of doubt that we dissected in the last chapters, to search for positive ways of seeing where God might be in doubt.

As already mentioned, Thomas Kuhn gave our generation a new language with which to talk about change - "paradigm shifts".[81] A paradigm shift occurs when a previously held idea or paradigm, on which a significant understanding of life has been based, gives way to a new framework of meaning and understanding. Paradigm shifts can be instantaneous or the result of a gradual build-up of evidence, information and experimentation that renders the previous paradigm obsolete.

Until the advent of Copernicus (1473-1543), Ptolemy's (90-168) description of the universe held sway. He said that all the planets, including the sun, revolved around the earth. Astronomical observations were based on this belief and theology found it useful for promoting ideas of the earth as God's field of activity and humankind the pinnacle. When experimental evidence challenged this scheme, additional rotations of planets *within* this system were described to accommodate new information but the basic model was not altered. Copernicus, however, was to revolutionize science by declaring that the *sun* was the centre of the universe and that the planets, including earth, revolved around it. This was quite a paradigm change. The way to think about the universe was turned upside down.

While Kuhn spoke of paradigm shifts in science, his model has far wider applications. A paradigm change occurs when a baby moves out of nappies; when a toddler realizes a parent will not always respond to a loud scream and when the dog exhausts its patience at having its ears pulled - and bites. There are later paradigm changes when a teenager realizes that money is earned, not distributed as pocket money, and that colleges do not employ mothers to make beds and pick up clothes.

In his book, Kuhn analysed the process of a paradigm change from the "accepted norm" to a new one. His steps help us see why we have problems with doubt in religion since doubt initiates these paradigm shifts and disturbs the status quo. According to Kuhn:

- Paradigms do not develop in a vacuum but depend on the cultural and scientific understanding of acceptable rules of the time.

- A paradigm serves as an adequate model until doubt and debate question its continuing usefulness. Such questioning initiates a paradigm change. Scientists revert back to basics to re-examine and re-apply the rules.

- Paradigm shifts result from the inadequacies of the existing theory and appear through routine scientific research or through crisis.

- Crisis occurs when anomalies become so great that the old paradigm is in threads before a new one emerges. The troops gather, the rules of normal science are broken, stereotypes are loosened and scientists even change the usual methods of research. There is a willingness to try anything, a plethora of emerging theories and a continual resorting back to the fundamentals.

- Even in crisis, however, science does not renounce one paradigm without accepting another in its place. This would reject scientific method itself because verification of the new paradigm depends on its comparison, not just with the world as the scientist sees it, but also with the old paradigm.

- All crises in science finish in one of three ways: (1) normal research finally proves it can handle the problem despite the initial threat to the old paradigm; (2) after trying everything, scientists set the problem aside for a generation with "no conclusion given current information and resources"; (3) the crisis ends with the emergence of a new proposed paradigm, together with an ensuing battle over its acceptance.

- Although there may be a number of people working towards a new paradigm, one approach will triumph and this new paradigm will be tested against, and applied to, all areas of research. For the new paradigm to be accepted over the old, it must prove to be a better model on which to base ever-widening knowledge.

- When a paradigm change occurs, scientists see new things in the old data. The old paradigm has not been updated or remodelled. Rather, a complete reconstruction of theories, methods and applications has occurred. The scientists use the same tools and language but employed differently in a new relationship to each other.

- The new paradigm does not have to explain all the facts that confront it — this is the job of continuing research. However, it has to be broad enough to allow for all these facts to be addressed.

- Once accepted by a scientific community, the new paradigm rather than the methods which produced it becomes the model for future research. This change may take a generation to complete if there is resistance and final acceptance of the paradigm is on the understanding that, although it may not answer all the questions, it provides a broader base, given current knowledge, than the previous paradigm.

- While most of the scientific community convert to the new paradigm, some will resist abandoning the old. These people often continue to work in isolation or join para-scientific groups.

Paradigm shifts are about shifts in authority. When a previous one no longer answers the questions, the new model becomes "authoritative". None of these models are "for all time" — each can become obsolete with changes in our knowledge, language and world view. We live with a succession of paradigm changes. By realizing this, we get a healthier understanding of "truth". Something can be true, in that it answers the questions for a particular period of time within a particular group, without being true absolutely.

This move from absolutes is central to postmodern thinking, allowing us to be more comfortable with change and uncertainty, but it is not new. The philosopher Carnaedes of Cyrene (approximately 214-129 BCE) doubted our ability to know "truth", claiming it was more realistic to live with probabilities as a guide for action, trying to determine which conclusion is more likely than another within the limits of knowledge. Interestingly for our discussion of "truth" in religion, Carnaedes denounced the form of argument he called *ataxia* meaning "heap", where people argue for truth, for example the existence of God, by piling a collection of different ideas and observations together which may not cohere into a simple system but become formidable as a heap. When you examine the different ideas within the heap one by one and disprove them, when is the heap no longer a heap Carnaedes asked? [82]

Whereas paradigm changes are part of all aspects of our lives and the doubts that initiate them are accepted as creative catalysts, paradigm changes in religion are fraught with difficulty. Why? Because in religion, "authority" and "truth" have been argued as absolutes with which we must not mess.   Perhaps the greatest paradigm change of all confronting Christianity today is what, if anything, can be called absolute and how much of what we believe is conditioned by culture and human input. Two major paradigm shifts in Christian history — the Reformation and the advent of the historical-critical approach to the Bible — have asked this question. The reformers questioned the doctrinal absolutes declared by the church for all time and post-Enlightenment biblical criticism challenged absolutes argued for the Bible under the umbrella of its literal inspiration by God, thus not open to question. Both these moves were initiated by doubt composted over time and both challenged the authority of a previous paradigm. Keeping Kuhn's steps in mind, we can understand how creative doubt played its part.

Paradigm changes do not happen in a vacuum. At the time when Luther, a faithful, disciplined monk, struggled with his doubts, the Renaissance had already challenged church authority, abuses of power and wealth by clerics were at an all-time high, and the printing press offered a means of communication to all people. In that volatile setting, Luther was unable to believe, despite his rigorous deprivation, that he had done enough good works to merit salvation. The "salvation by works and penance" paradigm, which was church teaching, was not working for him, yet he simply assumed that there was something wrong with him rather than the doctrines and waited a long time before he actually challenged the authorities:

> Although much of what they said seemed absurd to me and completely alien to Christ, yet for more than a decade I curbed my thoughts with the advice of Solomon, "Do not rely on your own insight" (Prov. 3:5). I always believed there were theologians hidden in the schools who would not have been silent if these teachings were impious. [83]

Finally, unable to squelch his doubts any longer, Luther's crisis sent him back to the basics. In the letter to the Romans, he found a new way to read the old words. He discovered that justification was not through good works but by faith given by God to the believer. This new paradigm was not an update of the church's teaching but a totally new approach to salvation. When he posted his thoughts on the door of the Wittenberg Church, he was not bristling for a fight but following accepted procedures for discussing new ideas by inviting debate with his colleagues. But his ideas challenged the authority of the holy Roman Church and, although his thoughts led to a paradigm change for the emerging "Protestant" traditions, the Roman Church simply re-affirmed and reinforced the old paradigm at the Council of Trent.

The importance for the Reformation was that Luther, like many of his colleagues who brought about this revolution, doubted. He could have prevented doubt from surfacing. He tried, as evidenced by his pushing himself to dangerous limits of austerity and self-deprivation because he saw his doubts as failure on his part. He could have jettisoned religious thought all together or simply conformed in outward motions. But he did not, because he knew through his doubts that somewhere there was more to "truth" and he was determined to experience it in a valid shape for him. His doubts tore him apart and threatened his belief systems. He looked for discussion with his peers, but the church was not hospitable to doubt since its authority was not open to question.

Luther's experience is like the experience many people have with doubt. A snag in one area of belief can crumble the foundations of a life-long belief system, threatening to bring it all down like dominoes. In science, such a crisis does not cause the scientist to throw all science out the window but to become more convinced there is another way to think. It is the difference between faith and belief again. When stories we have been taught to believe raise more questions than answers, we can doubt the story without losing faith in the sacred experience behind the story. Even if belief in a God is also in tatters, we can experience a drivenness within us that craves a relationship with something beyond ourselves, even if we cannot name that something.

To doubt and work through our beliefs is not to lose faith. Rather, it is like running away from home, knowing we can come back for dinner. It is like taking the phone off the hook but not disconnecting it altogether. It is like praying to ask if the object to whom we speak really exists. To deny doubts is to cling blindly to old paradigms that no longer make sense, yet we still do it. Such behaviour would normally deserve the label "magic", yet we do it. To eliminate doubts by jettisoning the old paradigm without replacing it with a new one is equally unproductive. Some throw out God because their human descriptions of God are no longer adequate — but that's another chapter.

Paradigm shifts are about choosing an authority — the old or the emerging new. In science, authority is established by experiment. In religion, "proof" is more elusive. While we could say the final authority is God, it is not so clear-cut because God always comes to us mediated, either by the church, by an interpretation of scripture, or through our own interpreted experience. Each of these mediatory authorities has been used as authoritative by differing groups at different times in church history. But when one form of mediation is claimed as the only true authority, problems with doubt arise. As French biologist and philosopher Jean Rostand (1894-1977) said:

> I am inclined to judge a belief quite differently according to whether it asks the right to be one or insists on being the only one. [84]

The Reformation was about challenging the authority of the institutional church. The reformers chose scripture instead as their authority, but while this paradigm shift may have solved the problem of a church hierarchy as the sole mediator of faith, it produced another authority conflict - in what way is scripture "authoritative"? The founder of Methodism John Wesley (1703-91) believed in a four-fold model of authority in religion - scripture, tradition, reason and experience. To decide what to do or think in a given situation, one reads what scripture says, considers the traditions of the church, thinks the issue through with one's own reasoning power and examines one's experience. This Wesleyan model of multi-based authority, however, does not satisfy all branches of Christendom. Some give priority to tradition, creeds and confessional statements; others consult scripture alone expecting "illumination" from the text; some pray then look for "signs", such as an appropriate text or unexpected event. One person told me that she once made a major decision because the brand of the shirt worn that morning suggested a certain choice. Medieval theologian Thomas Aquinas (1224-75) saw reason as the authority, with revelation from God provided only when reason was baffled. Today, experience as one's authority is returning to theology as a valid way of evaluating beliefs, having been banished from academia for years.

Different groups of Christians live under very different paradigms of authority, often unable to speak to each another because their basic premises are incompatible. This is demonstrated in the debate about the interpretation of scripture. While all see scripture as somehow authoritative for faith and life, in what way is it authoritative? Is it the actual "Word of God" as verbal dictation, or a collection of human words by writers trying to express the idea of God and the person of Jesus in their best images? How does one interpret various concepts in scripture outside their ancient but unique contexts? What is the genre of a passage? Should scripture only be read as factual material, like an operations manual, or have authors used metaphor and parable to tell the story? And how can we resolve all this two thousand years beyond the event? Should we even try?

There have been many different approaches to interpreting scripture in Christian history. The early church fathers saw secondary meanings in the texts - metaphors, allegories, moral stories. They certainly did not read all the writings literally and as historical events. They were also interested in the other written texts circulating in their communities that did not make it into the New Testament selection or "canon" of the fourth century, including many more gospels or sayings of Jesus. Some of these, e.g. the Gospel of Thomas, are being used widely by scholars today as a means of better understanding the New Testament's four gospels. We also need to realize that, in the early centuries, the followers of Jesus scattered around the Mediterranean did not have a collected-together New Testament. Rather, they had access only to whichever manuscripts had been copied for their community. Both scripture and church tradition were eclectic collections of poetry, visions, stories and allegories, as well as narratives, all genres familiar in their cultural setting and easily recognizable as such.

Until the Reformation, there was an open dialogue between tradition and scripture, each interpreting the other and informing the doctrines being formulated and reformulated by theologians. Both scripture and the writings of the theologians were equally valued guides to faith. However, when scripture became the only authority for the reformers, in reaction to church abuses sanctioned by tradition, there was a move towards a common sense interpretation of the Bible as authoritative, rather than the many-layered academic interpretations of the past. Even so, Luther did not accept all the books of the Bible as having equal value. He was unsure what to do with Revelations and unimpressed with the letter of James, calling it a book of straw because it advocated works as important for salvation, something Luther rejected. Of course, this selectivity and "common sense" approach was also culturally bound to what was common sense in the sixteenth century and, still today, some will argue that what was "common sense" for the theologians of that era is still true today, regardless of our changed context.

In the nineteenth century, an earth-shattering new paradigm for biblical interpretation emerged - biblical criticism. Rather than simply reading the scriptures as integrated historical narratives of an ancient people, scholars got "behind" the texts and asked questions about who wrote them, for what purposes were they written and from where did the source material for these writings come? From these investigations, the Gospels in particular took on a new face. No longer were they chronological, factually-historical records by eye-witnesses of Jesus, but separate essays compiled from different oral and written fragments of stories about Jesus, linked together into frameworks like ongoing narratives. Each Gospel had a particular theological point to make to a specific reader audience and this theme determined how the material was presented and what stories and events were included.

The writers of the Gospels were shown, judging by events referred to in the various texts, not to be the apostles of Jesus as had long been assumed and had dated the writings close to Jesus' life and death. Rather, the Gospels spanned a time-frame from 70 C.E. to beyond 100 C.E., and were addressed to different communities as faith statements of what each community believed, given their particular social and political situation. They therefore had to be read with this context in mind. Historical criticism dated some of Paul's letters closer to the time of Jesus than the Gospels and demonstrated that other letters attributed to Paul were composed by later writers following Paul's style and themes. As well as removing the authority of "eye-witness" accounts from these writings, we also have to consider the fact that we do not have any original manuscripts of these Gospels and letters — our earliest copies come to us several times removed from their original authors. We cannot know the totality of the correction and editing during that time. — but more of this later.

The work of biblical criticism continues to throw light on biblical interpretation and challenges the old paradigm of literal interpretation. Rather than every *word* being divinely inspired and dictated by master to scribe or recorded by eye-witnesses, this new paradigm allows us to recognize metaphors, political statements, extracts from liturgical formulae, re-interpretations of, and reflections on events, expansions of oral traditions and multiple perspectives on a similar event. Feminist scholars have more recently searched behind the words of the text to investigate the silence of women, comparing what is *not* said with other literary pieces of the time in order to recover and reconstruct something of the women's stories that have been lost or only reported from a male writer's perspective.

For example, scholars date the first letter to Timothy as early second century and not by Paul. This letter is concerned about false teachers and women's behaviour. We find scattered comments indicating that single women, whether widowed or unmarried, were claiming the right from Paul's words to stay unmarried and teaching this to other women in their homes — "gadding about from house to house ... gossips and busybodies, saying what they should not say" (1 Timothy 5: 13). "Avoid [such false teachers]", the writer says, "who make their way into households and captivate silly women" (2 Timothy 3: 6). Instead, "Let a woman learn in silence with full submission. I permit no woman to teach or have authority over a man; she is to keep silent" (1Timothy 2:11-12), a far cry from the women apostles and leaders in house churches that surrounded Paul. To further locate the "good Christian woman", the passage continues "[a woman] will be saved through childbearing, provided they continue in faith and love and holiness, with modesty" (v. 15). That there is in existence a second century manuscript, *The Acts of Paul and Thecla,* that describes a young woman refusing marriage to evangelize with Paul, illustrates this problem for a church now moving from Paul to conform once again with Greco-Roman rules of husbands over wives, masters over slaves and fathers over children.

Under the new paradigm of biblical criticism, permission is also granted to ask if words ascribed to Jesus were his actual words or themes remembered and interpreted by later communities. Thus we do not have to do theological gymnastics or claim divine memory recall to explain how Jesus' prayer of thirty-five verses, prayed *alone* in the garden before his death, is recorded in John's Gospel. Rather than each word being sacred, as from God, the general *theme* of the "gospel" or "good news" becomes important. Re-clothed in twenty-first century language and world-view, this "good news" can still speak to us despite cultural and linguistic limitations. A literalist will quote scripture verbatim, assuming the words meant exactly the same in the first century as they do today, or that God will magically provide a "simultaneous translation". A person operating under the new paradigm however will not assume meanings without allowing for the cultural, political, genre and linguistic differences involved.

This new interpretive paradigm of biblical criticism, about which I will talk more later in the book, gained strength in the nineteenth and early twentieth centuries. As in normal science, its methods were tested, debated and refined and have become the accepted tools for biblical interpretation in major theological schools today. But, just as in science, there are some who stay with the old paradigm and refuse to espouse the new, acting as if the Enlightenment and hundreds of years of biblical research never happened, or are simply false. The old paradigm of literal interpretation of scripture continues to be re-cycled and reinforced by fundamentalist TV evangelists who can read anything and everything into a few words of scripture under the guise of "prophesy". What is their authority? It is actually not "the Word of God" as claimed, but the interpretation of selective scripture by an authoritative preacher. It is a type of Gnosticism or "special knowledge". God no longer acts in the daily experiences of people but is mediated only through these evangelists who authenticate their revelations with phrases like "God gave me this special word tonight". Who is going to argue with that, especially if one is manipulated to believe that one's eternal destiny depends on believing it?

The problem with negativity to doubt comes when we are raised under the old paradigm and are not aware there are other options. The way paradigm polarization has occurred in Christianity, it is possible to live entirely under a narrow paradigm, even though unsatisfactory to one's sense of integrity, not knowing there are alternatives. When doubts arise, stock answers are given to defuse the doubt or to cause guilt to be internalized. These answers are not necessarily simple. They can be layer upon layer of detailed biblical explanation which sounds impressive and convincing but is spread on the same threadbare paradigm — like frosting on a cake that is stale.

Going back to Kuhn's stages in a scientific revolution, doubt can work as nudges in both normal and crisis of faith situations. In normal experience, we analyse anomalies and allow new paradigms to appear. Our doubts gently lure to broader faith experiences. However, when one's environment becomes fenced in so that normal processes of investigation cannot occur, the nudges of doubt produce crises. As in science where crises change the method of research and old rules are abandoned for a willingness to "try anything", crisis situations in faith allow us finally to move. In crisis, one is driven to the edge. We can reach a point where, to take the risk that there may be another "truth" for us or we may lose all our beliefs, is better than continuing with a charade. Uncertainty is better than any false certainty.

What if God is *within* this crisis as the lure to adventure rather than something against which we are rebelling? Questions labelled as dangerous under the old paradigm can now be examined. Theologians previously forbidden can be read. Prayer can freely acknowledge doubt and plead for new insights. Scripture can have meanings other than those prescribed. The Spirit can work with novelty and surprise. In crisis, God might finally earn a hearing. Answers can come out of crisis, but not without work, without struggle, without dark nights of the soul. This is part of the journey of faith. As Tillich said:

> How can [Christians] honestly say that they have no doubts about any of these dogmas? The element of doubt is an element of faith itself....One can never promise not to doubt. [85]

---

[78] Marjorie Suchocki, "Weaving the World" in *Process Studies* 14 (Summer 1985), 84

[79] Frederick Buechner, *Now and Then* (San Francisco: Harper & Row, 1983), 70

[80] Scott M. Peck, *The Road Less Travelled* (New York: Simon & Schuster, 1978, 45

[81] Thomas S. Kuhn, *The Structure of Scientific Revolutions,* 2nd edn. (Chicago: University of Chicago Press, 1970)

[82] Jennifer Michael Hecht, *Doubt: a history* (New York: HarperOne, 2004), 43

[83] Martin Luther, *Against Latomus,* in *Luther's Works*, Jaroslav Pelikan & Helmut T. Lehmann eds. 55 vols. (Philadelphia: Fortress Press; St. Louis: Concordia Publishing House, 1955-86) 32: 140-41

[84] Quoted in Bradley, Daniels & Jones, compilers, *The International Dictionary of Thoughts* (Chicago: J.G. Ferguson Publishing Co., 1969), 75

[85] Tillich, *A History of Christian Thought,* xli

Chapter 7.   "Are We Nearly There Yet?"

I am plagued by doubts. What if everything is an illusion and nothing exists? In that case, I definitely overpaid for the carpet. If only God would give me some clear sign; like making a large deposit in my name at a Swiss Bank.

Woody Allen (1935-) [86]

Life with children varies, but there are some stories generic enough to become bumper stickers. It is family vacation time. The children are up early, eager to leave. After a few false starts, the car is in cruise control half an hour out from home. Lunch time is four hours away, the evening stop four after that. A small voice comes from the back seat, "Are we nearly there yet?"

In previous chapters, we have seen doubts, not as negatives which condemn us but nudges that push us to move from one limiting paradigm to a new and richer one. In science, paradigm changes are slow and momentous, re-arranging the way humanity looks at its world. Some paradigm changes in religion have been equally major events as we have noted. But what about in our own little lives and histories? How does doubt move us from one stage to another? How many paradigm changes might we expect? Will we stop doubting? How do we know we have arrived?

James Fowler (1940-) in his influential book *Stages of Faith*[87] identified six stages observed in individual life journeys. Fowler based his work on the stages of personal growth described by Erik Erikson (1902-94).

Stage one: basic trust. God is a parent, a care-giver. Just as babies learn basic trust, so people learn basic trust in God. Strong principles of right and wrong about religion and guilt are indelibly written and children first meet the taboos by which families exclude unacceptable ideas.

Stage two: mythical-literal faith. One's thinking here is very concrete. Images of God are literal descriptions. Rules, both moral and spiritual, are stated. All is taken at face value with no shades of gray. Judgment mirrors the parent-child relationship with emphasis on authority and punishment.

Stage three: conventional faith. "I believe what my church or religious community believes". Faith is non-analytical and provides coherent orientation in the midst of other experiences. Valued authorities stabilize the beliefs with their opinion. There is a hunger for acceptance by peers and by God.

Fowler says that few people move beyond these three. Stage three gives them a defined belief package that needs little analysis and binds them together with others who accept the package. There are authority structures here — institutional church, creeds, human authorities and scriptural interpretations. Such a community may have the elements of manipulative suppression of doubt, as already described, or it may have the ethos of a Sunday social club with a pleasant psychologically uplifting sermon, an introduction to good citizenship and a belief system for children, with no demands made until the next Sunday. The theology offered does not threaten but rather creates feelings of warmness and security, allowing any secret challenges to belief to be ignored, often for a life-time.

Fowler recognizes however, that many *cannot* stop there. That experience of conformity and unquestioned security is as uncomfortable for some as the pea under the mattress was for the princess in the fairy tale. Doubts challenge the stability. The medieval crowd believed the claims of the emperor's new court designer, clapping and shouting approval from the side of the road. A woman probably tried to describe the outfit to her friend. Some folk may have thought, "I must be going crazy. I can't see anything but flabby flesh". But everyone else seemed sure, so the doubters waved their flags and cheered louder than anyone else so their suspicions could not be detected. Then the little boy cried out, giving permission to move into stage four.

Stage four: Individual and reflective faith. "As *I* see it, God is...". In this stage, one steps beyond one's earlier beliefs and is confronted with new ideas and new authorities which may be at loggerheads with previous authorities. We assume personal responsibility for opinions held and move from conformity to individuality. Doubt is the key that starts the engine, the tug of the boat that breaks the mooring, the wall switch that floods the room with light. In stage four, we distance ourselves from previous value systems and assumptions and receive permission to critically reflect. This stage often happens on leaving home, especially going to college where new, learned authority figures abound. It can be a frightening and disorientating time as we have left old security, but who would tell a bird not to fly?

In stage four, symbols, meanings, belief systems previously taken for granted, are questioned and stripped of unnecessary baggage to become more usable. The conflicting views of various authorities lead us to evaluate *all* authorities, trusting our ability to make creative choices and build a faith that fits, a new paradigm.   We walk no longer in the shoes of the other that cramp our feet, but in custom-made ones where we can wriggle our toes freely. We get caught up in details while trying our new wings — doctrinal minutia, problem texts, lengthy debates. We rewrite much of the script we have been using for years.

Transition to stage four is easier as young adults since this becomes one more factor in a complex time of fluid ideas. Sociobiologist E.O. Wilson (1929-) writes of going to college and being liberated from his literalistic beliefs when he learned about evolution:

> I had been raised a Southern Baptist, laid backwards on the sturdy arm of a pastor, been born again. I knew the healing power of redemption. Faith, hope and charity were in my bones, and with millions of others I knew that my Saviour Jesus Christ would grant me eternal life. More pious than the average teenager, I read the Bible cover to cover, twice. But now at college, steroid-driven into moods of adolescent rebellion, I chose to doubt. I found it hard to accept that our deepest beliefs were set in stone by agricultural societies of the eastern Mediterranean more than two thousand years ago. [88]

Fowler sees this change more difficult and painful for someone into their thirties, forties or older who has elaborate systems of relationships and roles established around the old paradigm. This late challenge may result from a relationship breakup or a move away from a familiar environment — or simply the maturity to finally address our questions, wherever it might take us. There is the possibility of throwing out both faith *and* belief, but a more common reaction in a late challenge is to preserve the work invested in one's life thus far and resist doubt, refusing to allow change. I am convinced many people staying at stage three are in this predicament. They are receiving the nudges but the old teachings represent security.

There is pain and guilt in moving to stage four if it entails parting with a previous allegiance or with family and friends who hold that allegiance. There is often a wilderness period with nothing yet firmly in place. There is doubt. But things do fall into line. More often than not, the new beginning "happens to" a person rather than something the person chooses. We may wake up one morning

> ....and realize that there is more order than chaos, more power to act than feelings of helplessness, more acceptance of self and worth than self-doubt and self-contempt....A stage transition is a painfully dislocating process of letting go and rebuilding. It means the dissolution of a way of being and knowing that was fairly stable and comfortable. It means living with ambiguity and a sense of uncertainty, often for a considerable period of time. It's no wonder that there is so much resistance to stage transitions, even when the present modes of being and thinking prove constrictive and stunting. [89]

Facing doubts, and thus moving into stage four, is like removing all the clothes from the closet and placing them back in a more functional arrangement. But such tidiness of theories and watertight systems do not anticipate all possibilities of life that continually track across our minds and leave footprints. When we recognize that life can be more complex and less watertight, and that theories may pale in the light of experience, we can move to stage five.

Stage five: the conjunctive stage. The individual has examined his/her beliefs in stage four and claimed new stories, perhaps somewhat dogmatically at times, but now realizes that all belief is limited in description and thus accepts "truth" as more multi-dimensional and open than any theory can explain. At this point, one can listen to other points of view without having to convert or be converted and is ready for dialogue with any who want to share a journey. Encounters with religions other than one's own are most productive here and one's commitment to ideologies will often be replaced with a concern for all people and conditions. It is the stage of irony with the ability to be content with one's own understanding for that moment, but also realizing that all understanding is partial and evolving; that certainty and doubt are always an evolving dance; and that that's OK. Nikos Kazantzakis (1883-1957), author of *Zorba the Greek*, described this stage of his journey thus:

> Always, whenever I reach some certainty, my repose and assurance are short-lived. No, doubts and anxieties quickly spring from this certainty, and I am obliged to inaugurate a new struggle to deliver myself form the former certitude and find a new one – until finally that new one matures in its turn and is transformed into uncertainty ... How, then, can we define uncertainty? Uncertainty is the mother of a new certainty. [90]

In stage five, we do not confuse the map with the territory. Whereas precise doctrinal map-charting was previously done in order to shape our world, we now put the map away or at least to the side and return to the environment it charts, the territory of our lived experience. We realize the limits of a map to fully capture the beauty of life. We also realize that symbols communicate beauty more powerfully than concepts and propositions. We move from dialogue as debate to dialogue as sharing, with an openness and confidence to allow each one's unique position.

Stage six: *universalizing faith.* For Fowler, this final stage is a little hard to define. The rare people in this stage have a special quality that makes them a living representation of the Ultimate. It is the quality we recognize in saints, a selfless passion given to the world in a particular moment for a unique purpose, a radical commitment to a vision for a transformed world, like a Gandhi, a Mother Teresa or a Nelson Mandela (1918-). For us ordinary people, I don't find this category very helpful. It is enough simply to recognize that there are exceptional people in life who burst beyond all our stereotypes and categories to leave their giant footprints in the world's sand while the rest of us continue to plod along.

Fowler's stages help us understand the movements from one source of authority to another that occur in life journeys. He also shows how the journey may move into loneliness for those who confront their doubts with courage. There is pain involved in letting go outmoded views or in leaving the comfort of the group. Only if we are totally convinced that "truth" is more important than security do we take the risk. Recently, I re-read some words I wrote long ago in a period when I sought a permanent "cure" for my doubts:

> To want so much to be in communion with God, this One
> whom I cannot see, cannot hear, cannot explain.

> To be prepared to give everything to God, to live for God's cause,
> but to be so unsure.
> I can see why people cling to rules and guarantees of salvation.
> There is no pain in weekly confession, in saying the rosaries,
> if it comes with an assurance
> that this mechanical, measurable action will guarantee the goods.
> It was so easy the other way of black and white, but now I am
> alone in the crowd,
> even in the midst of church committees,
> or a congregation at worship, God talk, action, prayer.
> I feel as alien as a blond in a Middle Eastern bazaar.
> What also worries me is knowing there are others hiding in this sea,
> swaying internally to the same drum beat as I,
> but still dancing to the music of the crowd on the outside.....
> Dancing so well, like me, that it is impossible to fault their steps,
> to spot an unfamiliar move, a hint that they too
> are wired to a call of a different kind.

Many will not take the steps beyond stage three and prefer to have their maps incomplete and outdated, to repeat the past rather than risk the pain and insecurity of major revisions in thought. M. Scott Peck said:

> What we do more often than not, and usually unconsciously, is to ignore the new information. Often this act of ignoring is much more than passive. We may denounce the new information as false, dangerous, heretical, the work of the devil. We may actually crusade against it, and even attempt to manipulate the world so that it may conform to our view of reality. Rather than try to change the map, the individual may try to destroy the new reality. Sadly, such a person may expend much more energy ultimately in defending an outmoded view of the world than would have been required to revise and correct it in the first place. [91]

Change is not merely the addition of a few new beliefs and the subtraction of others. Paradigm changes are about seeing the world from a different perspective, like a duck hunting magazine read from the point of view of a duck. Such a change affects all past thinking and understanding and challenges current views. We must be prepared to distrust all we already believe, all we hold dear. The religion of our parents is hand-me-down if we do not sift through it and allow our doubts to lead us to personal authenticity.

I work better with visual images. Fowler's stages evoke in me the image of a mountain climber. She struggles for a flat space on the cliff to rest. Her hands clutch a shelf for a moment and she hangs on, hoping no one will push the fingers away or her weight will not loosen the grip. When the plateau is reached, it is so narrow that a false move in any direction means a thunderous descent down the mountain. On the plateau, the temptation to refuse the challenge ahead, to hide from thinking about it, is huge. Yet the plateau is not a permanent place for a mountain-climber or a doubter. The slightest puff (or wind of doctrine) can dislodge. But oh, for a few moments rest before the tantalizing lure to see the view ahead pulls you up and on again. There is no guarantee of another plateau ahead, no indication of the height of the mountain, only that indefinable conviction that Something More is in it all.

Those who have been on the mountain slope will recall their unique experiences with plateaus and crevices. If all mountains were the same, all loose rocks and faulty ledges predictable, a guide map could be drawn. Some want to do this when they reach one plateau, believing their experience to be the only one. But they do not know that they never reached the top but rather are vegetating on a plateau a fraction of the way up. They sing and dance, oblivious that they have settled for a much lower view. Some take a chair lift and bid others do the same, avoiding the pain and the toil, but the chair lift only goes one route and also removes the experience of touching the stones and the moss, of inhaling the intoxicating smell of mountain air and the earthy smell of the soil.

I wake with a start from these poetic wanderings in imagery. A voice is calling from the back seat of the car, "Are we nearly there yet?" I am catapulted back into the old revival tent with the preacher shouting a third time, "Are you sure you are saved?" I hear a muscle-bound athlete (or was it a mountain-climber?) tell how once he was full of doubts, but now he had assurance and his doubts are all washed away. He has arrived! Well, perhaps not in heaven yet, but at least he is on the non-stop glory train.

You see the problem with metaphors like "stages of faith" and "mountain-climbing" is that, no matter how excellently they image our experiences with doubt, they also suggest a point of arrival where all doubt has gone. Such metaphors are basically linear, even if plateau experiences are described along the way. How many nights I cried out to God, asking for a "sign" or "experience" to dispel my doubts once for all - a flashing light, the sound of a divine voice, a touch on the face that would settle it for me so I could get on with the victorious Christian life. But the light, the voice and the touch never came. Now I am thankful, because had they come, they would have simply confirmed the second-hand belief system into which I was locked and I would never have continued questing and doubting and thinking and praying my way to richer experiences.

Fowler's description of the move from stage three to four corresponds to that decision to listen to our doubts and not be destroyed by them. This may be an instant in time or a slow realization. In many ways, it is the beginning of the dance with doubt. In this beginning moment, one still dreams there will be a time when all doubts are resolved, but somewhere, further along the way, perhaps at stage five, one suddenly discovers that doubt is a good dancer and leads the dance in ways that introduce richer moves. With this realization, one turns from the longing to arrive at the place where doubt is banished - "Are we nearly there?" - to an appreciation of the joy and adventure of the present in the interwoven matrix of doubt and faith. Zen writer Natalie Goldberg (1948-) says:

> There is no permanent truth you can corner in a poem that will satisfy you forever. Don't identify too strongly with your work. Stay fluid behind those black and white words. They are not you. They were a great moment going through you. A moment you were awake enough to write down and capture. [92]

Fowler's stages of faith represent different times in life journeys which *may* follow in some sequence of development but the metaphor becomes problematic and distorted if it is used to suggest a hierarchy of experiences or a linear progression ever upwards. There are times when one stage may be reached, but a crisis causes us to resist a further call to new experiences, to retreat back into the security of stage three. We probably all know of people (or have experienced this ourselves) who have ventured out on the path of new discoveries and faith experiences and are suddenly diagnosed with a terminal cancer or face the tragic death of a loved one. While they may have moved, in their more rational moments, beyond the theology of God allowing or causing such suffering for a purpose, they now need answers to the question "Why do bad things happen to good people?" and take refuge once again in the security of stage three where some authority will offer them certainty and the security of being "part of God's plan".

Having faith is to be "in process", living the present and trusting that, despite all the questions and doubts, there is something that makes one continue no matter how faint the light along the way. "Many of us", American journalist Bill Moyers (1934-) says, "move back and forth in the twilight of the mind where doubt and belief stroll together like old lovers … in the hope of getting to know each other just a little better".[93] Faith is not something noble and true and shining and brave. Just as often, faith is the fingers that clutch the rock, the last thing that saves the body from falling. Faith can be tattered and threadbare. It is learning to swim, trusting that, if our body begins to sink, something will hold us up. Faith says that, through my doubts, I am in process on the journey and it is the *process* that makes all the difference. Theologian Catherine Keller (1953-) says:

> How far I have become cannot be counted in years and miles. What counts is only the incalculable integrity of what I am becoming. [94]

---

[86] Quoted in Robert Cecil, Richard Rieu & David Wade, compilers, *The King's Son* (London: Octagon Press, 1981), 22

[87] James Fowler, *Stages of Faith* (San Francisco: Harper & Row, 1976)

[88] E.O. Wilson, *Consilience: the unity of knowledge* (New York: Knopf, 1998), 6

[89] Thomas A. Droege, *Faith Passages and Patterns* (Philadelphia: Fortress, 1983), 119

[90] Nikos Kazantzakis, *Report to Greco* (London: Faber & Faber, 1973), 338

[91] Peck, *The Road Less Travelled,* 46

[92] Natalie Goldberg, *Writing Down the Bones* (Boston: Shambhala, 1986), 33

[93] Bill Moyers, quoted in Chandler W. Gilbert, *Seed Pods and Periscopes: stories and reflections about living deeply and living well* (Jaffrey, NH: Charred Pencil Press, 2008), 119

[94] Catherine Keller, *From a Broken Web: separation, sexism and self* (Boston: Beacon Press, 1988), 248

Chapter 8.   Doubt and the God Question

To live fully is ....to become so absorbed in something or someone as to lose all sense of time and space. It is the travelling towards rather than the arriving.... It is gratuitous grace.

Charles Birch & John Cobb [95]

Ever since the prodigal son stormed out of the house, the image of journey has featured in church literature.   A journey is undertaken for at least two reasons: to enjoy the view along the way or as a necessity in order to arrive at a destination. If the purpose is the former, we concentrate on each moment as an event of value in itself. If the purpose is the latter, the "getting there" is something to be tolerated, even endured or suffered.

The way we choose to use this metaphor for our life with reference to God depends on both where we imagine God to be and what we imagine God to be. Is God experiencing with us in each moment on the journey? If so, the relationship with the divine is "in the now". Or, is God something standing apart from us, a little way ahead, or beckoning from where the road disappears into the horizon, or even looking down from on high in the clouds above the road? If so, God is our goal at the end of the journey. God's location is certainly not straightforward. In church school, we sang in the same morning that "There's a friend for little children above the bright blue sky" and prayed that Jesus would "come into my heart". We sang about God watching and hurting over each little sparrow that fell to the ground in God's beautiful earth, then prayed longingly to escape this world of sin and woe to be with God somewhere else.

The questions of whom or what God is, where God is and how God acts in the world are crucial for our understanding of doubt. These questions are responsible for the majority of religious doubt. We may get hung up on details of theology, such as whether and how the resurrection happened or whether Jesus was born without a human father, but the overriding creator of doubt is the question of God and God's existence.

If the whole point of the Christian faith is something called a relationship between God and us, then it would seem centrally important to know the form and place of residence of the other in this relationship. Confusion exists here. We speak randomly of God, Jesus, and the Holy Spirit all juxtapositioned in one sentence. Some people seem to have a preferred personal image, overworking the Spirit; some see magical efficacy only in the "name of Jesus"; while others refer always to their good friend God who sounds rather like a best-friend-forever in a teenagers' magazine. All this demonstrates, not a fine-tuned knowledge of Trinitarian doctrine, but a downright uncertainty about what's what.

How we describe God *matters*, because it determines how we relate to the Divine and live our lives accordingly. As to the question of doubt, our personal image of God also determines whether we can believe in a God at all. Some readers might become squirmy at this point as I raise the "elephant in the room" for many doubters, but much religious doubt finds its roots in the valid question of whether God exists and, if so, in what form and shape (a full discussion of this can be found in my book *Like Catching Water in a Net: human attempts to describe the Divine*).[96] For most of us, we have been offered only one what-the-Bible-says description of God and then told to believe it. However, the Bible does not give us a unified portrait. We first meet a wind-like Spirit brooding over the waters, then "the sound of God walking" in the Garden of Eden. A cloud and a pillar of fire portray God in the wilderness wanderings, followed by a divine warrior slaughtering everything in its wake to protect a chosen community, despite also being a God of love and justice. Other biblical passages describe God as a mother hen or brooding eagle protecting its young, but most Christian art down the centuries has simply painted God as a grey-bearded man, usually ruling from a heavenly cloud, thus defying anyone to think of God as female, non-gendered or without human form at all.

Because of such art and the Trinitarian language of Father, Son and Spirit, we have, despite hundreds of other biblical images, fished from a miniscule pool — God as a ruling male, whether father, king or lord. This selectivity makes ordinary people assume that these are the predominant biblical images and thus the correct way to imagine God. Yet the Hebrew people were specifically forbidden not to do this. In Deuteronomy, Moses reminds his people what the divine Voice said to them as part of the covenant:

> Since you saw no form when the Lord spoke to you at Horeb out of the
> fire, take care to watch yourselves closely, so that you do not act corruptly
> by making an idol for yourselves, in the form of any figure — the likeness
> of male or female, the likeness of any animal that is on the earth, the
> likeness of any winged bird that flies in the air, the likeness of anything
> that creeps on the ground, the likeness of any fish that is in the water
> under the earth. And when you look up into the heavens and see the sun,
> the moon and the stars, all the host of heaven, do not be led astray and
> bow down to them and serve them (4: 15-19)

We've been able to ignore this command by making the verse refer to stone
images or other objects we worship, but it was much more than that. It was
a warning to human pride against imagining that we could know what God
is or picture God in any form.

With their inability to explain scientifically the wondrous workings of
the natural world, the Hebrew people could accept a Creator as unknowable
mystery, but listening to some preachers today, they seem to know exactly
what God thinks and how God acts in every instance and can almost give
you God's vital statistics. However, as we learn more and more about our
immense and ever-expanding universe, any God-language about a
"Creator" must make sense within this knowledge, not over against or
separate from it. We can no longer describe God's activity in the world in
ways that contradict what can be scientifically demonstrated as the working
of natural laws.   Scientists tell us that there are more stars in the universe
than there are grains of sand on earth, thus any description and form of
God has to be big enough to encompass such a universe if it is to make sense
in today's world. God as a human-like Being in the sky sending floods to
punish some and finding car parks for the faithful needs serious rethinking
— as do many claims we have made about Jesus. This is not something
dastardly action of a doubter. It is the responsible action of any thinking
person. Theologian Sallie McFague (1933-) says:

> God is embodied in one place and one place only: in the man Jesus of
> Nazareth ... The source, power and goal of the universe is known through
> and only through a first-century Mediterranean carpenter. The creator
> and redeemer of the fifteen-billion-year history of the universe with its
> hundred billion galaxies (and their billions of stars and planets) is available
> only in a thirty-year span of one human being's life on planet earth. That
> claim, when put in the context of contemporary science, seems skewed, to
> say the least. [97]

The key to any discussion of God is the reality that anything we say about God are metaphors — images that are not descriptions of the thing itself but something borrowed from our culture and experience to help us envisage the thing otherwise difficult or impossible to describe. In the beginning of recorded biblical time, the Divine was imaged as powerful objects from the natural world - wind, water and thunder. However, as the wandering Hebrews settled into communities with a powerful leader, the leader imagery helped to imagine God — king, warrior or father of a clan. The problem with any metaphor is that it is culturally bound and time warped. God as a shepherd (Psalm 23) was an excellent image of divine protection when one's livelihood rested on a flock of wandering sheep on the rocky ridges of Palestine. However, the average child in Sunday School today has never seen a shepherd — and some have only seen sheep in picture books! Unfortunately, many people continue to use ancient metaphors for God "because they are in the Bible", thus making the *metaphor* sacred rather than the mystery it tries to describe. The doubter is right, therefore, in challenging the status quo in order to interpret this Mystery for our time.

In theological terms, divine location and action of this Mystery have centred around the terms "transcendent" and "immanent".[98] Like any other terms, the meaning has evolved through history. Transcendent has, in general, meant anything beyond our human bounds, independent of history, not affected by it but affecting it, the "totally Other" to humanity. Transcendent does not have to be an elsewhere location but rather complete freedom from time and space, not confined to our limitations to understand or describe. Immanence, on the other hand, can mean close by or within, an integral part of us or of nature. These terms are not mutually exclusive because it is the limitless of transcendence, the ability to be anywhere and everywhere, that enables something transcendent to *also* be near or within. The God of the Hebrews was imminent in that God spoke and acted within the day by day struggles of the people, but this immanence was only part of the transcendent God of everywhere, the Divine freedom. When King Solomon built the first temple in Jerusalem in order to "locate" God somewhere within the Hebrew world, he was conscious of this difference — "But will God indeed dwell on the earth? Even heaven and the highest heaven cannot contain you, much less this house that I have built" (1 Kings 8: 27).

When the Jerusalem temple was destroyed in 70 C.E., the symbolic location of God-with-us was also destroyed. Our gospels were written after the destruction of this temple and in them we find Jesus described metaphorically as the new temple, the new location where we encounter God-with-us within the man Jesus. What Jesus' followers experienced of God-with-us in Jesus, they also encountered, after Jesus' death, as the Comforter, the Spirit also dwelling in them. In time, however, the Hebrew working God who acted in history became the Greek image of a totally other God residing in the mists of heaven, all-powerful and all-knowing. Seated beside him high on the clouds was the exalted Jesus through whom this now remote God could only be known, while the Spirit was the part of the Trinity active within the world. This immanent, free Spirit, however, was now domesticated to work *only* within the church as messenger of the elsewhere God and Christ, thus the triune God could only be known through the church. Transcendence now had the meaning of removed, as opposed to immanent as present. Of course, there were always those who did not subscribe to an inaccessible God mediated only through priests and sacraments — the mystics claimed to encounter God for themselves in an immanent relationship, hence their threat to Pope and church. Throughout history, the institutional church and the mystics have embodied the ends of the continuum between transcendent and immanent God, between heaven and earth, between sacred and secular.

This dualism continues to be reflected in Christian thinking. The idea of God as totally other and of different substance from us reflected Greek dualism between mind and body, spirit and matter. Activities of the mind or spirit were prized, while the functions of the body despised — a human parallel with the superiority of the sacred (heavenly) over the secular (earthly). As an aside, according to Greek philosophy, men contained considerably more spirit than matter and women more matter than spirit, a dualism that projected inferiority onto "bodily" women. Sexual desire was linked to the body and women became the temptresses who veered spiritual men from their course, justified by a reading of Eve as the original temptress. Asceticism was the goal and, by the Middle Ages, an all-male priesthood, celibate, as least in name, mediated the gap between the sacred and the profane.

While the language of the New Testament talks of a kingdom or reign of God *within* and Paul claimed that Christ lived *in* him, we have worshipped a God "up there". The doctrine of the Trinity, while trying to account for what fourth century church fathers saw as various modes of God, also reflects a struggle with divine location, with transcendence and immanence. Prayer is still raised upwards to a God in the heavens, in accord with the medieval view of the three tiered cosmos - heaven above, earth in the middle and hell below the ground. Science has disproved this simplistic universe but we still raise our eyes and hands in prayer as indication of where God is. Michelangelo's (1475-1564) famous painting in the Sistine Chapel of the outstretched finger of God reaching down from the clouds to Adam representing humanity, fingers never quite touching, freezes forever the image of separation — the elsewhere, unattainable God.

We also unconsciously perpetuate this dualism by talking about our "spiritual" life, "spiritual" growth and "spiritual" journey, indicating that these are somehow different from our ordinary life and evolving maturity. Actions and feelings that directly relate to God, or have a pious ring or a good feel, qualify as *spiritual* life, while a simple walk down to the mailbox on a beautiful afternoon in Spring is a secular experience. One of the most over-worked and under-explained words in our vocabulary today is "spiritual". Everybody uses it for a variety of experiences yet few define it with clarity. The term has become a way to talk of anything which goes beyond the material mundane. Even if we don't always know how to define it, the fact we use it to differentiate from the ordinary is an indication of our continual emphasis on duality.

Since the first edition of this book, "spiritual" has gained even greater usage as an alternative to "religious". Because so many people are disenchanted with institutional religion and its dogmas, whether Christian, Jewish or Hindu, saying we are spiritual rather than religious acknowledges that we sense Something More in the universe but do not see this authentically described in religious traditions. While this does free us from ascribing to religious dogma whose use-by-date has passed, it still maintains the dualism between sacred and secular, between some spiritual realm and ordinary life resulting from our ingrained concept of God as a Being writ large somewhere "out there".

This is not the understanding in this book. We are whole beings, living very much and very deliberately in a physical world, arms, legs, head, spirit (whatever we mean by that) all making up part of one whole body. Our journey is our *life* journey which includes all aspects of who we are, every experience we have. Feelings, spirituality, doubts, physical pain, are not different levels of being. Every mundane, uneventful, frightening, joyous, loving experience is a total event in which, if we believe in a God, must also include the divine at work. God is therefore in a hug of a friend, an awareness of a stronger glow in an early morning sun, the unexpected epiphany of the beauty of a butterfly wing, as well as in a sermon or prayer.

As I have said before, this challenges us to rethink God. Most religious doubt is around traditional ideas about God and how God acts in the world. Science has challenged medieval descriptions of our cosmos which included descriptions of God's location. It has also shredded ideas of a divine telephone operator in the skies taking our calls requesting this and that and interfering with the natural laws of the universe to send earthquakes on offenders and miraculous healing to the faithful. Although the traditional religious art in most of our churches still depicts God and Jesus as two men in the heavenly clouds with a bird-Spirit as messenger between heaven and earth, we are invited to fish more widely for God-images that make sense within our evolving view of our universe. In what way can God be imaged as source and life within our world?

Such is the question with which contemporary theologians struggle. "Theology" is described as talking about talk about God, recognizing that talk about God has changed through the centuries, influenced by scientific, social and cultural knowledge and experience. The job of the theologian is to constantly investigate such talk to see what holds true in a different or evolving scientific, social and cultural setting. It is to challenge the church to change its doctrines and images of God if they demand head-in-the-sand obedience to a previous era. Theology has never claimed a single image of God but rather has evolved through the centuries. The problem for doubters is that such evolution of ideas has not always been offered to those of us sitting in the pews.

As far back as the early Greeks, the philosopher Heraclitus (535- c.475 BCE) said that we can never step in the same river twice. He meant that the basis of reality is change and flux - all is in process and constantly moving on. Western thought did not follow Heraclitus, however, choosing instead Parmenides (early fifth century BCE), who said that, behind change, there were more fundamental realities that endured. Western philosophy thus spoke of static concepts of "being", "substance" and "essence", rather than dynamic concepts of "becoming", "process" and "evolution". Thus the church fathers, in trying to formulate the creeds in the fourth century, had a problem when they tried to describe the relationship between God and Jesus using this philosophical understanding of the day. How can one talk of two different "substances" in the one person? The creeds finally did, but more as a faith statement about mystery than a proven conviction of how this could be. They were working within the current known categories of how things were, thus we have inherited their doctrines of the "essence" of God, the "natures" of Christ and the "substance" of the bread and wine, even though we have moved beyond the philosophical framework in which these doctrines were conceived. [99]

We are operating within a new world-view today, scientifically, culturally and socially. We find that life is more about dynamic activity, about events and interaction, about interconnectedness, flow and change, which not only impacts us from the outside as one bumps into the other, but also involves internal relationships. In this model, everything affects everything else and is affected by it. Thus, to be in relation with something or someone is to be internally changed by that relation. Now we *know* that we do not step into the same river twice because our world is not the same twice and we are not always the same "substance" but constantly changing.

Just as the church fathers used prevailing philosophical concepts to explain the meaning of things, changing world-views have spurred on philosophers to develop new philosophical paradigms to match the changes. Let us look at one such paradigm. In the first half of the twentieth century, with the collapse of Newtonian physics, mathematician and philosopher Alfred North Whitehead made the move from "substance" to "event" thinking in order to propose a philosophy that incorporated all elements of knowledge, including God and science, into a single language framework without dualisms. Since science was demonstrating the universe to be an interconnected organism in constant flow and change, Whitehead proposed that any God-talk should also be able to be described within that framework, not separate from it or of a different "substance". Whitehead, in critiquing the exclusiveness of scientific thought in his day, said:

> The reason for this blindness of physical science lies in the fact that such science only deals with half the evidence provided by human experience. It divides the seamless coat — or, to change the metaphor into a happier form, it examines the coat, which is superficial, and neglects the body which is fundamental. [100]

Whitehead's popularity has increased after his death because his philosophical framework (Process thought) goes hand in hand with postmodern thinking. Although Whitehead did not set about to prove or disprove a God-idea, his philosophy is useful for theologians because his scheme *allows* a space for something Christians can call God, not external to or separate from us and our world (a duality), but an integral part of the universe. Whitehead wanted to account for human experience, nature — and what some image as God — as part of a common genus rather than different characteristics, thus God must fit into this non dualistic framework where everything consists of the same basic entities or events. The question of God can therefore be discussed with scientists within this framework, rather than in opposition to science.

Whitehead postulated that everything in the universe is composed of a series of "experiences" or "actual occasions" (events) which are not a continuous flow but discrete events that follow each other, the previous event having causal efficacy for the one that comes after it. Everything that exists, from God to a piece of fluff, can be explained in terms of a series of events. The sum effect is that we are not an enduring substantial "thing" from birth to death, with any change as accidental and not really part of who we are internally or at our core, whatever that is. Rather, we are a multi-layered series of events happening faster than our consciousness, each of which changes who we are from one moment to the next. All the many events that make up who we are at any moment, however, are not necessarily "sense" experiences i.e. ones of which we are conscious. Changes happen constantly in our cells without our conscious knowledge, yet we only have to look at how we grow and change in any moment to know all this is happening. A human being is not just one series of events but a multiplicity of events at any one time taking place in the brain, the digestive system, the emotions, all contributing to the process of becoming who we are at any moment.

Each emerging event "feels" the event immediately preceding it, selecting from that past event what it wishes to incorporate into the present event. As an event perishes, a new one is emerging. While the emerging events "feel" past events and select from them, that is not the sum total of information that constitutes the becoming event, otherwise each event would only repeat the past. For each becoming event there is what Whitehead called a "subjective aim" that organizes *how* the new event will become. The "initial aim" of this organizing principle is what theologians using Whitehead's scheme call the God-activity in every event. This "initial aim" (God) suggests the maximum possibility for the realization of each event. God, also described in "event" imagery, can "feel" all experienced events in the world (including each of us as a series of events) because, as any event perishes, it becomes part of the "objective immortality" of God. Nothing of life experience is lost to God but becomes part of God's ever-growing experience, and is available to be "felt" by events in creating further events.

All the events of which we are made could accept this initial aim for each event in each moment but do not, because things tend to cling to the past. However, when the events that are us *do* accept part or all of the potential or novelty offered in each event, this moves us to richer experiences. The more we are open to embrace God's optimal initial aim for each moment, rather than modifying it by past experiences, the more we become "like God". Thus we talk about who we are, not as who we were at two years old, but as what we are becoming with each moment of possibilities for greater richness of experience. What makes us the "same" person over time is our memory - we can remember experiences of childhood even though we do not consist of the same cells we were then or even the same thoughts. Although beyond the scope of this brief discussion, such series of events happen in every interconnected thing in the universe, not just human beings.

This is the tip of the iceberg of Whitehead's scheme of things, but it does describe a way in which God can be at work *in* us and in the universe. God is no longer the transcendent God who exists unto the divine Self, alone and outside of history, only intervening from a position in eternity. It is more like the biblical Spirit of John's Gospel — the Spirit that was in Jesus and now in his followers. Nor is this pantheism where God *is* everything, flowers, rocks, bugs, but rather that which is *in* everything yet *more* than the sum of all the parts — panentheism. This is that which works *in* us — what we have called "God" — affecting and affected by what happens to us, yet also that which is within the whole universe of all interconnected things. Whitehead sees these two aspects of God for which he uses the terms "Primordial Nature" of God — the abstract aspect of God beyond us in which all possibilities for the world exist — and "Consequent Nature" of God — that which presents the best possible 'initial aim" for each new moment of existence.

Since we do not always take up the fullness of the suggested aims but settle for something less, God is *affected by* our choices and subsequent initial aims can only be formulated within the limited options our choices have helped to create. The initial aim is always the *maximum* possibility given the *limits* of the moment. While we are determined to a certain extent by our past and can still choose to repeat it for each new moment, rejecting the novelty offered, we also have the freedom to choose novelty. Thus we are not "determined" by God but rather lured towards a choice, within every cell in our body, for greater richness of experience and greater freedom. We are co-creators with God and God is affected and suffers with us when we make choices which pain others and God. God does not therefore "cause" suffering but is affected by what our choices produce, as we are.

This description of divine action as "God within" us and everything in the universe though not limited in any way by this is a far cry from the Being upstairs sitting on a throne, directing the fortunes of the world from another location. You can perhaps sense how I struggle, therefore, with the term "God", as it conjures up a certain image and mode of operation however hard we try to think otherwise. Because of this, some people no longer use the term "God" with its masculine, anthropomorphic shape, choosing terms such as God/ess, the Mind of the Universe, Love, Life. These terms image the Divine as the integrating power of the universe, Source, Life, Energy of all that is and Mystery about which we struggle to speak. In this book, however, I will continue using the term "God" as a symbol, along with other terms, while recognizing all its difficulties. [101]

It may be becoming clear how this model of divine action, as both the transcendent God of pure possibilities and the immanent God at work in our lives and in the world, helps to understand creative doubt. Doubt emerges at the interface of each becoming moment when the possibilities presented for richness challenge our temptation to repeat the past. Doubt surfaces in light of this "suggestion" that there is a richer way to think and act than previously experienced. Even if we choose at first not to step out and accept the lure of divine suggestion, this possibility can be introduced in future moments when we may have incorporated more information into our world-view to enable us to respond to our doubt and step out, trusting God's lure.

In this Process model, doubt is a sign of maturity not weakness. It is the ability to "hear" the divine invitation to adventure. "God in us" is also a different type of power relationship. The traditional view of God is an omnipotent Being who determines what is to be, a patriarchal Head, Father and Judge. The Process model of God is one of enabler, persuader, not one who forces. Thus we do not need to ask of this God why God causes or allows suffering. This God offers us maximum possibility for each moment, yet we are free to choose otherwise. Since our choices all constantly impact each other and internally affect each other — and God — in this interconnected organism, our world, choices against the optimum aim will also be causal for the suffering of others — and God. Perhaps the most helpful image for such interconnected living is that of a web. When someone tugs a strand on one side of a web, no matter how small the strand may be, the whole web shakes and must stabilize itself to hold together. Process imagery puts God *into* the structure of this web, thus God is also affected by the tension.

Like all other descriptions of mystery, Whitehead's model is a metaphor, a way to describe something otherwise difficult to describe. No metaphor claims to be "truth" itself but rather offers images that help us imagine something beyond human vision — it has to be "helpful" rather than provable as "true". It has to better accommodate our experience of the world. In the imagery of our journey of life, God is no longer up there, out of reach in the heavens, intervening with periodical zaps but not actually experiencing the pain of the world. We are no longer "aliens" on earth, walking quickly and alone between birth and death, watched "over" by a God who may seem simply to be moving players on a gigantic chess board. The world is not the enemy to be avoided or converted, but the good creation in which, as ongoing co-creators, both God and us are living, breathing, connected workers. Divine Energy is with us within creation, eternally present in the world. How can we feel strangers on this stage and how can we continue to desecrate it, working against the divine desire for the harmony of the whole creation?

If God is with us now, this challenges a focus on the future. Our journey is to be present in each moment, to choose freedom and richness from the limitless possibilities offered in each particular moment. If we have the freedom to choose or reject richness, the future is being created in the present. This is where Process theology differs from traditional understandings of the future. In earlier days, predestination thinking pictured a giant plan drawn up by God which not only determined everything each of us would do on this earth but also identified those "elected" to be saved. Later theologians questioned this idea, especially in light of other biblical texts which indicated God willed all should be saved. More recent thinking, which still holds some idea of a great plan, allows for *some* freedom of choice in the everyday moments, but a determined future as our hope. Process thinking prefers to concentrate on our present co-creating with God, out of which we can trust a future will emerge but not a predetermined one — the future is always open.

What we think about the future affects our description of the journey. If the whole point of life is a place in a future heaven, a clean slate, obedience to a set of rules to get there, then the journey of life is simply a means to an end. This ordinary life is incidental to the *real* life - the "spiritual journey". This spiritual journey, as opposed to our ordinary life, can take varying shapes, depending on how we get started on the highway and how we stay on it through to the heavenly gates. The *point* of such a journey, however, is not the process, but *arriving* at the end - as the hymn says, "Earth is a desert drear, Heaven is my home". When destination-oriented living is combined with progressive moral and spiritual improvement, the spiritual journey becomes an escalator ride to heaven, oblivious or disdainful of the dust and dirt under our feet — "I'm pressing on the upward way ..".

While the goal is agreed upon in such future-centred theologies, there is a variation of opinion as to where this "spiritual" journey begins. For many, a conversion experience is the point of entry to the freeway, with the "once saved, always saved" group seeing the only freeway exit as Heaven, although one may stop and mess around a bit on the road. Some see the freeway covered with glaze ice. The chances of sliding off are extremely high, thus the need for lots of rules and techniques to remain on track. Believers in predestination enter the freeway at conversion, but with a ticket gate on that entry ramp allowing only pre-registered members through. Catholics began the journey at birth, with regular Sunday forgiveness check points along the road.

In contrast, the moment by moment process of responding to life's nudges and lures, of choosing greater options rather than being bound to repeat the past, is the point of the journey. *Right here* is where we are in relation with the Spirit within, each other and our world. Each choice for greater richness in our lives is also a choice for richness for all. Such a concentration on the present while remaining open to what the future may bring is not to deny the future. Every choice in the present *is* also a choice towards a richer future. What that future will be is open because we are continually co-creating the future with God. This thinking is in line with the contemporary world-view that sees an open future, depending on choices in science and technology, politics, ecology, and global harmony. Today's discussion about climate change is all about how our choices affect the future of the planet, as do our negotiations together for peace. But what does such openness say to the person who wants a future all spelled out, to be achieved by following a set of rules? Does this present-oriented thinking give the cold shivers to someone who needs to know that there is a heaven, exactly how it will look and the steps necessary to get there?

The way of living that concentrates on God's relational activity in our present and trusts the process for the future, whatever it might be, is "faith". It is not about answers, assurance of heaven, fear of hell but about *living abundantly* in every moment. When the focus of life's journey is on arriving successfully in the future, living abundantly in the present is trivial and fraught with tension, since present events are simply "read" as indicators of the future — why does my life not go smoothly? Why do I doubt? Why do I have detours, rock slides, and often lose my way? Why don't I feel more spiritual? What does this mean in terms of my salvation? Will I get to heaven?

Future-oriented living is like playing a game to win. I remember the cold feeling in my ten year old stomach when, two squares from HOME in Snakes and Ladders, I slid down a snake and had to start over. In Monopoly, the aim was to pass GO, collect $200, accumulate much wealth and property along the way and avoid being dispossessed of your gains. The winner was the one with the straightest run, the least number of obstacles and the greatest number of chances.

Those who live for the future see the "Christian Life" as winning the final prize. Another theological student became quite frustrated with me one day in our American seminary when I suggested that America's obsession with competition, with winning and losing, with being number one, produced more emotional damage in the many losers than positive personal experiences for the few winners. I had cited the devastated faces of those who lost in professional sports, whose life hopes had been gambled on a win. The student read his written response to me in the next class in the form of a letter, asking me to do some serious reflecting on why I was so passionate in my arguments. Describing the World Series sports event, he said:

> The World Series would be nothing without competition...It is pure contest, focused on the rules of competition. The point is to win. Why were the millions of fans enthralled by the contest? We could say that baseball aficionados watched to appreciate the good baseball. But baseball is played well only in order to win. The skills of throwing, hitting, catching, pitching, and base-running serve no other purpose other than winning a game according to the rules laid down for the game. Now winning is what we all want to happen to us ultimately. Winning is symbolic of our destiny. And the experience of winning even as spectators of a sporting event is an ecstatic experience. We are caught up outside ourselves in an experience that gives us intimations of a larger unity, a final "winning".

I *did* do some reflecting. I thought back to biblical images used for the "race" of life. One image bids us to run with patience the race that is set before us, looking to Jesus the author and finisher of our faith (Hebrews 12: 1b-2a). In another, Paul is quoted as saying that he ran the race, finished the course and kept the faith (2 Timothy 4:7 - although we now know this was not written by Paul). I was thankful for that invitation to reflect because it led me to even better examples of what I was trying to verbalize. These words are not about winning or losing as the goal of the race but about the race itself, about patience and persistence and faith in the running. Our place in the end — first, second or last — is not significant. It is enough to finish, knowing that in the *process* we have "kept the faith", whatever that means for us.

All this allows us a theological framework for doubts to become adventures, not moments of terror. Our journeys will be unique, given the unique combination of circumstances, opportunities, hazards and nudges, a uniqueness that is not some measure of our "holiness". For some, the life journey may be a straight path from birth to death, no detour signs, no bumpy roads, no ambiguity. Such a smooth journey may *also* indicate little risk, little openness to adventures into which God lures us. To repeat the past is to opt for certainties. It may make for a quiet life, but it gives little chance for adventure and passion in living.

Those who live with an openness to doubt and challenge see their journey more as a spiral, winding in widening circles of questions and answers, but still advancing to greater richness. It may be a slow process. Each revolution through doubt has to be thoughtfully resolved. When one question is navigated, there is another waiting to be addressed, often with no lull time at all. Doubts may not let us rest if we have committed ourselves to honesty. When we cry "enough!" or turn back from the nudges, the internal lure does not cease. If we block out doubts, new, irresistible clues cross our path. Many ask what God's will is for their lives. God's will, written into this model of divine urging towards richness, is that we doubt, question the blind yet safe repetition of our past, discover, grow and push back the barriers we create to protect us from risking something new. Anyone who has struggled constantly to suppress niggling doubts will know how repressive this state of mind can be, how limiting the struggle to "just believe" really is.

The Divine with or within us changes the understanding of prayer. The image of a frantic heavenly telephone operator manoeuvring plugs on the switchboard to keep us all on the line is no longer helpful! Prayer becomes an internal conversation (or voiced out loud) born out of shared experience, the attuning of oneself to choose richness offered in each moment, a dialog in our inner being. To raise our hands in prayer reinforces old concepts of a God *not* with us on the journey, a God somewhere else that needs enticing to attention. Instead, each becoming moment as we are open to that within us and the universe *is* prayer. We cannot hide our doubts because God is participating in them, perhaps causing them to move us on. I recall the frustration and defeat I used to feel as a child, knowing that the doubts that squirreled around in my head could not be squelched but could also not be concealed from the all-knowing God. What a recipe for constant defeat and inadequacy.

Some people seem to be able to accept everything they hear, taking it on board without question. Others, whose personal intellectual honesty or whose need to test evidence prevents such compliance, cannot "just believe". This is not a "good/bad" grading but a fact of life because we are all different. One person might climb into a car, turn on the engine and drive off. Another checks the tires, the fuel indicator and the brake light, then takes off. Each is a step of faith that cars can move. If both are sound, the outcome is the same and neither driver is better or worse off. If both are not sound, one driver will discover the fault and make adjustments before the trip, while the other may have an accident. Even if the one who checks does not find a fault, thoroughness produces an inner knowledge and assurance that the vehicle is road-worthy.

This has been my experience with belief. Doctrines that many people seemed to accept happily sent me into a long process of checking texts, reading books, talking with others, thinking, debating and pondering long into the night. Sometimes I came to comfortable conclusions. At other times, having exhausted all arguments (checked all the car's systems), I did what my other friends had done initially — take the step of faith, but not blind faith because I had explored all aspects humanly possible and found belief reasonable even if not "provable". Belief is the goal in each case but the path to belief is different. For some, the authority of another is sufficient for imitation. For me, belief came after I personally worked through the pregnancy, confinement and labour to "give birth" to new understanding. Sometimes this process can take years, a holding pattern with no guaranteed arrival. "Going round in circles" can be difficult, yet is part of the journey. The writer T.S. Eliot (1888-1965) understood this:

> We shall not cease from exploration and the end of all exploring will be to arrive where we started and know the place for the first time. [102]

The roads of the Austrian Alps are punctuated with mountain tunnels. Many are short with no time to feel claustrophobic. Some are quite long. Once driving these mountains, having passed through a series of short tunnels, we entered another, automatically adjusting to a few minutes of darkness. But the tunnel went on and on. The car's headlights searched repetitive arches of concrete for an exit. After a while, a foreboding came over me. The image of being caught in a pitch-dark eternal tunnel from which there is no emerging, yet no way back, clutched my heart with icy fingers. Naturally the story ends happily, but such long tunnel experiences are real and nightmarish on the life journey, long stalemate where answers no longer seem to come. All of us have tunnel times, even though we are loath to admit it, and when one tunnel ends, we can be sure there will be more.

When we look at our life journey as a process, winding roads are also OK. Four lane highways may seem fast and uncomplicated, as long as you stay awake with the boredom. Winding roads allow time to see finer things, visions lost on the fast lane. Highways are easy because all the hazards have been eliminated. Trite answers, set formulae, answers to prayer and exuberant belief smooth the potholes. Perhaps because one is confident that there are no bumps on a doubt-free highway, one can break an axle or blow a tyre, totalling the vehicle with the smallest challenge to belief. Winding roads need concentration and alertness but such awareness in the moment also allows the scenery to be experienced.

If we continue a journey metaphor, Process thinking allows for exploration of the side roads when the highway becomes blocked. The major motor ways north of London are victims to dense fog and, predictably each year, massive pileups cut off the north of England for a period. Travellers resort to winding roads through villages. If all we know are simple straight answers, we have no map of alternate roads, no contacts off the mainstream of our thinking and thus we cannot do anything but stay still, hoping the fog will clear or that something will rescue us. Groups that control their theology by isolating people so no one can glance sideways at other opinions force people to stay on one road whose signposts say "Only Way", leaving no options for a struggling doubter.

A final journey image for our ongoing process of doubt, beliefs and faith is the temptation to sit on the side of the road when the fog of questions comes. In Process thought terms, this would be to resist doubts and continue repeating the past, including past feelings of inadequacy under oppressive authorities. We see no other way to go, no other path. We may also do this when we are so beleaguered with responsibilities that we do not have time to attend to new ideas. Either way, we keep moving our legs but marking time, going nowhere. To deal with questions takes time, especially if there are no mentors to help find satisfying answers. The temptation is to put the struggle on the back-burner and fill one's mind with other things.

A professional friend told me her story. She had been raised with a set of beliefs one *must* accept. When her adult experiences, both in her studies and career, challenged this belief system, she did not know where to find answers for her doubts. The local pastor preached doubt as a negative and her devout family could not fathom why she had problems just believing. Family visits were uncomfortable because she was quizzed about her "spiritual state". Her husband had left his inadequate belief system without much trauma and wondered why she could not do the same, but she had made a thorough job of internalizing guilt and blame for her "problem". She continued to attend church, even though each visit made her feel more and more alienated. Finally, she quit church, resolving to live with her guilt.

Overly busy with work and family, she balanced everything, yet in fleeting quiet times the questions would return to haunt her.

When we met, she assumed I accepted the traditional religious teachings because I was studying theology, so she avoided any conversation about beliefs. One day I made a critical comment, rejecting some doctrine I had read about. My criticism was one of the questions she also had! The flood-gates opened and she talked for hours. I could understand her experiences exactly, could finish her sentences when she was stuck for ways to describe the agony, because I too had lived through blaming myself for doubts, praying for assurance, only to find more doubts. She was amazed as I described portions of my journey almost word for word her experiences.

We were together only a few days but it was enough. When she left, she felt like a free person, not because she had dealt with all her questions - that was no longer the immediate priority in her frantic schedule. Rather, it was because the load of guilt had been removed. She had received permission to step out of her prison of self-accusation into a more liberating way of living. She could work on theological details at her own pace later. For now it was enough to know that God was "in process" *with* her and that her doubts were healthy reactions to the inadequate belief system of her relatives. She was on her way, confidently jotting down questions with anticipation to think through later. The pain had gone, that desperate feeling when personal experience *refuses* to fit prescribed belief. She had learned that faith is not knowing all the answers or all the questions, and that that is OK. In the following years, she has read whatever she can find of contemporary scholars and writers who also encourage her to ask the questions and find new ways of thinking.

There are tensions in accepting new thinking if the old ideas are still held dear by those close to you. This is especially the case with a path different from one's parents. But choices must happen for authentic living, just as children choose careers, lifestyles and partners different from their parents. To follow one's own journey is not to negate those who continue on the path you have left. Their journey is authentic for them and their beliefs are valid for them. We need, rather, to celebrate together that we *each* have found experiences right for us, our *own* story.

> A journey, years ago, has brought each of you through thick and thin to this moment of time as mine has also brought me. Think back on that

journey. Listen back to the sounds and sweet airs of your journey that give delight and hurt not and to those too that give no delight and hurt like hell. Be not affeared. The music of your life is subtle and evasive and like no other. [103]

Each life journey has its own original detail, an autobiography on foot. By living our experiences, our story becomes more real than any book or testimony. No one event in the journey is more significant than others or represents the one and only "before" and "after". The well-worn line of the hymn "I once was blind but now I see" may work for some but is certainly not the universal experience. God works the divine magic from the start of life, thus every moment has a before and after. Our unique blueprints of the journey thus far are drawn by our past. We compare each new experience with this blueprint and recognize it as an opportunity for novelty - a divine moment. Our blueprint is thus enlarged and incomplete notes jotted down earlier fall into place, making sense at last. *This* is the meaning of incarnation - the divine Presence *with* us on our journey.

Jesus wrote nothing down. Perhaps he knew that faith must grow in each individual through his or her unique experiences. Jesus taught about the reign of God using examples from lives of ordinary people around him. This is still the way to see God's ongoing incarnational activity in the world - through contemporary experiences of everyday people, you and me, discovering nudges of divine grace and acting on them.

Today's mass of How-To books outline a problem and then offer a solution. I waited many years to put these thoughts down on paper. I was waiting until I had the solution to doubt, waiting until I could head a chapter "the answer". But I do not have *the* solution to doubts. Solutions indicate finality, resolution. Too many solutions are peddled in today's religious bazaars - guaranteed steps to happiness, spirit-filled highs, various formulae for victorious living. Rather, I believe the solution to the struggle with doubt, beliefs and faith is to *be* on the journey, to accept the continuous becoming of the road. There is never the moment when I will say I no longer doubt, because doubting brings new answers which bring new richness of experience and thus new questions — and so it goes on. To have no more doubts is to no longer be truly alive.

In the introduction to Russian writer Leo Tolstoy's autobiographical *A Confession and other religious writings*, he wrote of his Orthodox upbringing against which he struggled with his doubts:

> Judging from various memories, I had never believed very seriously but had merely trusted in what I was taught and in what was professed by my elders; but this trust was very unstable ... religious teaching, which is accepted on trust and sustained by external pressure, gradually weakens under the influence of knowledge and experience of life that stands in opposition to the religious doctrines; a person can go on living for a long time imagining that the body of religious instruction imparted to him when he was a child is still there, whereas it has in fact disappeared without leaving a trace. [104]

---

[95] Charles Birch & John B. Cobb Jr., *The Liberation of Life: from the cell to the community* (Cambridge: Cambridge University Press, 1981, 1984), 109

[96] Val Webb, *Like Catching Water in a Net: human attempts to describe the Divine* (New York & London: Continuum, 2007)

[97] Sallie McFague, *The Body of God: an ecological theology* (Minneapolis: Fortress Press, 1993), 159

[98] For a larger discussion of God's location, see chapter two in my book Val Webb, *Stepping out with the Sacred: Human attempts to engage the Divine* (New York & London: Continuum, 2010)

[99] For a further discussion of this, see Robert B. Mellert, *What is Process Theology? An introduction to the philosophy of Alfred North Whitehead, and how it is being applied to Christian thought today* (New York: Paulist Press, 1975)

[100] Alfred North Whitehead, *Modes of Thought* (New York: The Free Press, 1966), 154

[101] In my book *Like Catching Water in a Net: Human attempts to describe the Divine,* I have used GOD to continually remind readers that the term God is actually a three letter symbol for the Divine or Mystery, free from the traditional connotations of religious art.

[102] T.S Eliot, quoted in Dan Wakefield, *Returning* (New York: Doubleday, 1988), 158

[103] Buechner, *The Sacred Journey*, 77

[104] Tolstoy, *A Confession*, 19

Chapter 9.   Independent or Interdependent?

The web of interaction is what we are starting to weave together. Let us imagine the radical choreography of all sentient beings.
Catherine Keller (1953-) [105]

The usefulness of any metaphor depends on how well we define its limits. Since a metaphor stands for something else, it is not the same thing as what it signifies and in many instances may only describe one aspect of what it stands for. Thus the metaphor of the personal journey, while it is a useful way to talk about our life experiences in this world, it is not a complete picture.

In past chapters, I have talked about a change in thinking from people as autonomous individuals to the interconnectedness of all things including non-human living entities, changing each other internally through interaction. We are part of a whole, an interwoven web, an organism of many parts, droplets in an ocean. Perhaps only a hermit in a cave on an isolated hill can travel his life journey with any sense of aloneness. Yet, even there, he is interconnected with the atmosphere and the elements, with the animals and food plants of his solitude and even his consciousness of avoiding others connects him with those others. I have rejected a metaphor of journey that existed only for the goal, opting instead for journey as being present with God in each moment of the process. Yet, even in these personal moments, we are not alone, since each moment can only become another moment by incorporating into it some of the many influences present with us at that moment.

This image of a multiplicity of events impacting us as choices in any moment — that "radical choreography of all sentient beings" — conjures up a vision of riotous activity as each jostles for attention. This multicoloured dance would explode into infernal confusion of competing discordances except that, in each moment, there is the calming urge of the divine Lure, aware of maximal possibilities and persuading us with an optimal choice within the din. While we may not be open enough or free enough in ourselves to choose perfection in the commotion of each moment, the offered Life possibilities give an ordering that allows us, even imperfectly, to make choices towards richness rather than disharmony and stagnation.

Doubts are also present in the life dance of each moment when novelty is offered and doubt urges us not merely to repeat the past. Whether we want to call this persuasion to be open to change by the term Life, Mind of the Universe, or God, this power is at work in each and all of us in this interconnected choreography. It is this inner urging that creates the doubts that move us into new territory, nudges from God clothed in many different forms and carried in many different vehicles within the whole.

What then do doubts look like? How can we recognize them as the positive shoves towards adventure that they are? How can we make ourselves available to these nudges? Doubt may come as a fleeting thought that skims through the mind like a diving swallow, leaving an imprint of flight that will not go away. Doubt may surface when an image of a dusty, weary Jesus trudging towards Jerusalem superposes itself in our minds over an ecclesial procession of ornate vestments and glittering gold. Doubt may nudge us at the sight of the Grand Canyon at dusk, defying any taming of earthlings and whipping our breath away to challenge us not to settle for mediocrity. Or doubt may be the little boy who asks the "he's naked" questions. Doubts can't be predicted, but can be recognized as crazy, holy grace if we are open to the possibility, rather than the sign of dastardly unbelief. Often, it is in retrospect that we better identify doubt as the internal mechanism or engine that allows any faith to emerge, even if fleeting. Australian social commentator Hugh Mackay (1938-) says of the more general life setting:

> Our doubts serve us well. Doubt drives the healthy scepticism of voters who mistrust the cockiness, the unjustified confidence and glib promises of politicians ... Living with doubt and uncertainty can sharpen your understanding of what is at stake ... The world is a complicated place and easy answers generally turn out to be inadequate. Doubt, if not actually chic, is a perfectly acceptable position, especially when all the evidence is not yet in. [106]

Before we go too far with concrete examples of how doubt might appear as a necessary tool in our interconnected lives, the two words "experience" and "feelings" - terms loaded with double meanings - should be clarified. Evangelical conservative and fundamentalist type Christianity bases itself on what is called a personal experience of God through Jesus

Christ. The tenor of testimonies, emotive hymns and passionate pleas suggest a conscious and continuing emotional "experience" or "feeling" as, not only the desired expectation for the genuine Christian life, but also the measure of one's grading in divine eyes. Yet, in reality, it is also a rather rationalistic and cognitive form of religion where one makes a decision of the will by assenting to a set of propositions about the Bible, God, and sin, regardless of one's feelings and even if this does not line up with one's own life experience or everyday living. In fact, the message is also to distrust one's first hand reactions to life as the heart can deceive us (Jeremiah 17:9).

Theologian Virginia Mollenkott (1932-) describes how, as a soul-winning graduate of Bob Jones University, she would ask persons who "came forward" in revivals to repeat a certain statement prayer after her, but also assured them that they were born again even if they did not "feel" any different after the prayer. While this reassured those expecting flashing lights, the convert later encountered the expectation that a "personal experience" of Jesus Christ *should* produce an element of supernatural "feeling" (emotion) through the presence of the Spirit. This gave one "assurance of salvation" and its absence was often the result of doubt or lack of faith.

Author Frankie Schaeffer (1952-) is the son of Francis (1912-84) and Edith Schaeffer (1914-), Calvinist Presbyterian missionaries who founded L'Ábri, a retreat in Switzerland for conservative religious thought. While Frankie was involved in this ministry with his parents until mid-life, he moved beyond such teaching and embraced the Orthodox Christian faith. In Frankie's wonderful novels and memoirs, he tells of growing up where doubts were suspect. His mother had none — only his father had doubts. The children knew this because their mother told them that their father's faith was not as strong as hers. All his father ever said was "I wrestled before the Lord while walking back and forth in the hayloft of Chalet Bijou in Champéry, for many days and nights on end. I was ready to give it all up. I questioned everything!" [107] Of course, such a confession by Schaeffer senior, the guru of a generation of conservative evangelical young people, was only made after he could attest to have *conquered* doubt. Of his novel *Zermatt*, based on his family, Frankie Schaeffer says that evangelicals who stumble on this novel don't like the fact that the missionary father is portrayed as losing his faith – "If life can't be tied up in a neat package, if you let those doubts begin to gnaw at your guts, where will it end?" It is no coincidence, Schaeffer says, that 99% of evangelical books are written about how to keep your faith in spite of sex, food, exposure to new thoughts at college, etc. – "in other words, in every breath you take".[108] It becomes a denial of life in order to toe the path of dogma.

While raised in a similar tradition, Mollenkott earned her Ph.D. in literature and was expected to give the same scholarly critique to the Bible as she gave to other literature. It took courage because she was afraid the whole basis of her belief system would collapse. Her religious interpretive grid *did* collapse, but out of this collapse of beliefs, she discovered faith. She distinguishes between the quiet holistic experience of faith and the noisy rationalism of mere belief.

> Fundamentalism is rationalism that cloaks itself in the language of experience. When a person has an authentic faith experience, he [she] is able to listen with an open mind to diverse points of view without feeling threatened. But if a person's world view is based only on rationalistic belief in an airtight, limited, pre- packaged belief-system, then the better the evidence that somebody else introduces about an alternative approach to reality, the greater the distress - and the more necessity for a Bible-thumping insistence on absolutes. [109]

When Process, Liberation and Feminist theologies talk about "experience" as the basis of theology, this is a different use of the term. Here it refers to the first-hand experiences of everyday life that inevitably shape what we think about life — and about God. The way we image God *matters* as it determines the way we live our lives. If God is the giant policeman in the skies checking to see if we believe dogmatic "truth" even when unbelievable, we live our lives in fear of offending and suppress our doubts and questions. If God is the divine Spirit urging us from within, we become co-creators with this Spirit and our experience should be trusted as it is *lived* experience, forged through listening to our doubts as divine nudges.

As an example, for centuries the church taught, courtesy of a few biblical verses, that women were inferior, the originators of sin because of Eve, weak of mind and unable to lead men. Because of this supposedly biblical injunction, all sorts of restrictions were placed on women and they were virtually rendered powerless except for serving men. Women were told to believe the dogma, even though this did not fit with their experience of life. Not until the last century did women challenge this theological rule because their *experience* of life showed them otherwise — perfectly capable of doing whatever men did and more than able to be leaders in their own right. In the same way, Liberation theology emerged in South America when the poor, having previously believed doctrines that kept them poor and subordinate, paid attention to their experience of poverty and revisited the Bible, finding many references to the poor as God's special concern and Jesus as focused on their liberation and need for justice.

As for feelings, even though new converts from mass revival gatherings may be assured at that moment that they may not feel immediately different, this is paradoxical. Such evangelism gatherings are programmed to induce highs by external means, not unlike scenes from rock concerts. Music, atmosphere and hype are specially chosen to produce an emotional feast which, once created, is labelled the Spirit at work. Waving hands, vibrant colours, elaborate stage design, shouting, pleading, repetitious demands on God and the sinner are orchestrated towards the final drum roll when emotions are at their peak. Does the Spirit need such a build-up to work? Must God be summonsed with the trumpet blast, by demand of the faithful? Or are these props rather to ensure human success and head counts? When the crowd and shouting disperses and one stands in the midst of the debris, where is the Spirit then? Must we look for another high, another meeting, another praise session?

Feelings do not come from God as *proof* of one's possession of the Spirit, as many doubters have been taught. Feelings are our human responses and can also depend on what we eat, the amount of sleep we have had, the weather and our mood. If feelings were indicators of God's presence or acceptance of us, when the feelings ebb with natural bodily functions, so would our assurance of divine validation. This would hardly be comfortable teaching for women whose monthly cycles could cause havoc with such a spiritual barometer! Feelings are our human responses when, in some concrete everyday moment, we catch the sudden, elusive, fleeting unexpectedness of recognizing, not just harmony but something behind or within that harmony. Feelings can come in a quiet, cool forest when, with footsteps silenced as sound is drawn into the earth's breast by the moss underfoot, an erratic bird call, sometimes distant, sometimes as close as the mind, pierces the silence. Feelings are evoked when the eye, seeing only the interwoven green cover for long minutes, suddenly reels as a detail springs into sharp focus - a filigree leaf, a moss covered branch, a lace embroidery of lichen. Such moments are responses of feeling and emotion to this experience of something bigger than us, an interconnectedness with the whole, opening a crack to let transforming light shine on the ordinary moment.

Feelings as our response to God are random and unpredictable. There are moments when reflection on divine action brings overwhelming feelings of joy, warmth, relief. John Wesley encountered this in a moment of illumination when he comprehended for the first time a wider dimension of faith and felt his heart strangely warmed. He never claimed a permanent warm heart as an indicator of God filling his soul, nor did he indicate that God acted only when Wesley experienced such a feeling. Interestingly, it was Wesley who added a fourth leg to the stool of how we can know about God. Previously it had been scripture, tradition and reason. Wesley added "experience", not the emotional experience or feeling he had when his heart felt warmed, but experience as down-to-earth life experience, the everyday circumstances in which we find ourselves and in which we "recognize" divine involvement. This has been called Contextual theology — thinking about God from within the specific context in which we live, the everyday situations experienced in which God has to be "good news". God is not good news for the wretchedly poor if nothing is done about their lot and they are told simply to put up with it "for your reward is in heaven". God is not good news for those unjustly imprisoned if they are simply told it is God's will.

The issue of feelings is important where doubts are involved. Feelings have been billed in the past as barometers for spiritual certainty, suggesting doubt and feelings bear an inverse ratio. We need to realize that feelings are erratic, even fickle, and serve, not as a given for true faith, but as an ice-cream treat on a good day. We all know that we can have good feelings in many situations, including those when we know we are actually doing something that we should not do! Doubts, instead, are the workers, the catalysts that allow a new end-product to be formed in a chemical reaction. Feelings are the bodily created optional extra, like the unexpected enjoyment of a pleasant aroma as a side effect of the chemical reaction.

Feelings in religion are like feelings in love. Contrary to what true romance novels say, people do not spend their whole life consumed with erotic passion in each other's presence. Total absorption may be the scenario in courtship, but if this went on forever, nothing else would get done. People have to move beyond living in this cocooned emotional hothouse stage in order to work at *real* love where both grow independently and interdependently as well. There may be times when feelings of love are not present, when one wants out but hangs on because of a shared commitment with a person that goes beyond feelings at any moment. If there is no commitment beyond an emotional high, there is no will or incentive to keep going.

The experience we call faith also has its dark moments of the soul, the winters about which the saints wrote when God feels distant or absent, but we cling to the conviction that God *is* (or is that the divine Urge clinging to us), despite our feelings. Something in us tells us that something is there, makes us shout out in anger in the loneliness of our room, makes us beg for a sign and drives us to cry in our pillow night after night because the curtain seems drawn across our access to God. Many do quit or shut out their own internal cries, refusing to listen. Others struggle on, driven by that intangible, unreasonable intuition that there is something with which to connect.

In this book, I use "experience" and "feeling" in Process theology terms. Experience is everyday living which can be tasted, seen, heard, touched, and spoken. God - or however one wants to name or image that something - is in each experience and event. We "feel" God in each event, not as emotional tingles but in the sense of exploring the novel possibilities presented to us, like feeling for a fit before choosing, whether we are conscious of doing this or not. So many events happen within us of which we are not conscious — we only have to think about the incredible organism we call our bodies to know that much is happening just to keep us alive minute by minute. In some rare moments, however, we may "feel" an interaction with the Divine, an "a-ha" experience that produces a wave of emotion, often in retrospect. Such moments are cherished, but they are not moments when something is present as opposed to absent.

> The question is not whether the things that happen to you are chance things or God's things because, of course, they are both at once. There is no chance thing through which God cannot speak - even the walk from the house to the garage that you have walked ten thousand times before, even the moments when you cannot believe there is a God who speaks at all anywhere. [110]

Process theology has given us tools to imagine the Divine as working with us within the universe, rather than God as the stern judge on high demanding we believe what the Queen of Hearts in *Alice in Wonderland* called "six impossible things before breakfast". However, there are other ways to talk about or imagine God that also free us from guilt about our doubts. Many people today say they are "spiritual" rather than "religious" because they sense Something More in the universe but do not want to be associated with a stagnant church or outdated doctrines to be believed and not questioned. They have listened to their doubts and walked away from the traditions, finding other ways to experience the Sacred within the world.

What has become known as the Progressive Christian network around the world, consisting of many people who stay associated with their religious denominations, and many who do not, has challenged traditional doctrines about God, original sin, Jesus, the Trinity and salvation, focussing more on Jesus as a wise sage intent on bringing a message of justice through a longed-for reign of God; and on what we have called God as Mystery, not to be imprisoned by human concepts and language. This is not an unreasonable position since the fourth century councils from which our church creeds emerged were still debating, three hundred years after Jesus, whether Jesus *was* God or *like* God. Some of the best contemporary scholars in theology and biblical studies support this movement, offering different explanations to the life and work of Jesus such that the doubter is vindicated rather than condemned for having raised the same questions. Such openness allows for, even encourages doubt, as it leads us to better knowledge and experience.

Many others have moved beyond institutional religion and a personalized divine Being to live with the mystery they call Life, Love or Ground of Being, hesitant to describe further that which they experience as operational in the world. The tragedy for centuries has been that people within many Christian congregations have not been told about such scholarship and theological developments and have been forced to sit in pews, churning inside with obvious but unanswered questions. Not surprisingly, a new handbook on Progressive Christianity takes up this very point in its title, *We Weren't Told!*[111] With all these different ways of thinking, doubters have a choice to follow their doubts in directions that best address their questions, rather than simply being locked into "correct" answers.

With imagery that envisions something we can call God operating within the pulsing universe as novelty or potential for life in every moment, let us see how nudges that encourage us to doubt the status quo can lead us into richness rather than condemn us to hell. Doubts appear when we become aware of a discrepancy between what we are taught and what we experience. They invite us to readjust our thinking such that the discrepancy is no longer a roadblock. The nudges of doubt can come as unexpected thoughts or images in moments of solitude or equally through people and objects that constantly interact with us - books, sermons, conversations. Like the next stepping stone in a rushing stream, they appear when there seemed no safe place ahead to put the foot. We are lured and persuaded where our attention will best be captured — in ordinary events in which we are most often absorbed and alert.

To many, the universe itself generates powerful emotions and so nudges may come through nature since we are already attentive to its magnitude. Each unbelievable colour combination on an insect's wing, each obscure stage of a plant's life cycle, each Arabian Nights perfume from a Cinderella weed, each clumsy act of love in the animal species, each sequential shade of colour on a mountain at sunset — all these can initiate the drum roll for a sacred nudge, opening us to a new future. Natalie Goldberg described this beautifully:

> Our senses by themselves are dumb. They take in experience, but they need the richness of sifting for a while through our consciousness and through our whole bodies. I call this 'composting'. Our bodies are garbage heaps; we collect experiences, and from the decomposition of thrown-out egg shells, spinach leaves, coffee grinds, and old steak bones of our minds comes nitrogen, heat and very fertile soil. Out of this fertile soil bloom our stories and our poems. But this does not come all at once. It takes time. Continue to turn over and over the organic details of your life until some of them fall through the garbage of discursive thoughts to the solid ground of black soil.[112]

For those who find magic and message in the printed word, we can be nudged to move beyond the present through the writings of those who dare to bare their souls. While many people today do not take time to read much, especially in our contemporary society saturated with social media, the internet and television, others find the printed word an enchanted kingdom, a world in which to lose oneself in imagination and contemplation. I fall into this category. At each major crossroads in my journey, there has been a significant book that helped bring my doubts to speech, navigating me through rocks into new waters.

Perhaps this realization finally convinced me to put *my* thoughts down in print. Such writing takes courage because what we write today will not be what we think in ten years time, yet our words remain etched in stone. When British journalist and religious writer Malcolm Muggeridge (1903-90) was interviewed years after his book *Jesus Rediscovered* was published, he acknowledged that his thoughts had changed, but he was not concerned because any book, once published, takes on its *own* life as a conveyer of thoughts.[113] It speaks by itself, regardless of whether the writer still personally holds to all its thoughts. This is exactly the meaning of the interdependence of all things. Muggeridge's book was created out of his experiences at a particular stage of his life but his book has become an entity in itself that is able to nudge thousands of people who are now entering that particular stage of the journey. Years after it was written and, no doubt, when Muggeridge was in a different place himself, that book was a highlight on my journey, his words falling clearly and soothingly on my ears like Oxford English in a room of foreigners. It nudged me to embrace my doubts as valid and put me on the path to new discoveries.

The above paragraph was written seventeen years ago in the first edition of this book. Now, as I write this updated edition, I am faced with that situation about which Muggeridge spoke. Seventeen years and five books later, I have developed new imagery and language about God and new ways to describe my journey. I have also long accepted doubt as a healthy and creative companion on my way. Religious doubt has also become more acceptable with books in the public marketplace by Bishop John Shelby Spong, Professor Marcus Borg and other scholars who have also championed doubt as a catalyst to liberating thought. However, I must remind myself that, for readers that have not yet experienced freedom from guilt about their doubts, my words of seventeen years ago that offered liberation for the doubter in that time will continue to offer liberation today. In these seventeen years since this book was first published, I have regularly received and still do receive letters from people who have just found the freedom they sought through this book.

How wonderfully liberating it is to discover a book that mirrors your own personal journey. American naturalist Henry David Thoreau (1817-62) said:

> How many a man has dated a new era in his life from the reading of a book! The book exists for us, perchance, which will explain our miracles and reveal new ones. The at present unutterable things we may find somewhere uttered. The same questions that disturb and puzzle and confound us have in their turn occurred to all the wise men; not one has been omitted; and each has answered them, according to his ability, by his words and his life. [114]

A Chinese proverb tells of a hyperactive little boy whose teachers tied him up to the door post of the temple. His toe was still free to move, so he drew mice with it in the dust. The mice were so life-like they came alive and chewed at the ropes until the boy was free. Another person's experiences, though they may be just trailing sentences on a page to someone not at that place on their journey, are like mice to others, coming alive and setting them free.

I can map significant moments in my life journey with books that were nudged into my hands when I needed them. The fascinating thing, and the reason I believe strongly in doubt as grace, is that all the books appeared in crazy, unpredictable ways. Malcolm Muggeridge's writings only found acceptance in the theological confines within which I was moving in earlier days because he was a *convert* from atheism to Christianity — a coup for the Lord! While the content was certainly not all kosher with the group, Muggeridge's approach suggested to me that perhaps there *were* other ways to think and I was also introduced, through him, to two other authors, French philosopher Simone Weil (1909-43) and German theologian Dietrich Bonhoeffer.

Bonhoeffer's book *Letters and Papers from Prison* was earth-shattering for me.[115] His journal entries from the final days before his execution by the Nazis reflected on his religious doubts arising out of this crisis. They addressed questions I had long asked, offering explanations that affirmed me at that moment of my life. Others may read this book and be less affected and, when I reread it today, the impact is not the same because I have internalized his thinking and used it to move on the new places. But, at that moment, it was as if Bonhoeffer spoke directly to me. Although he was frowned upon as a "heretic" in my Christian group at that time, I had somehow *discovered* him through Muggeridge.

At a time when I began questioning the origins and politics of the New Testament and the church creeds, I found Bamber Gascoyne's (1935-) book, *The Christians*.[116] The discovery was as profound as follows — the book was on a dollar table at a book sale. I remember even debating that dollar since I had not heard of the author and didn't know his "angle". However, since I was doing some teaching on Christian art, I decided that the illustrations were worth the dollar, even if the text was not. Gascoyne's unholy humour about the church fathers gave me my first permission to loosen up over biblical literalism and understand the humanness of Christendom — and perhaps even hear a divine chuckle as well.

At another moment, I was questioning the divinity of Jesus. I had read many books, to no avail, as each sidestepped or waffled over my particular questions. For no reason, a friend gave me a catalogue of recently published books and one was listed called *Jesus*, written by Catholic theologian Edward Schillebeeckx.[117] I knew nothing of this writer then, but the précis of contents posed my exact questions and so I ordered it. My congested head, cluttered with Christological arguments, none of which satisfied me, cleared like sinuses before a vaporizer. Although *Jesus* was difficult and long, it didn't matter because Schillebeeckx was gathering up for me, step by step, all the threads dangling loose in my mind. Soon after, I discovered fellow Catholic rebel theologian Hans Kung's book *The Christian Challenge*.[118] It was incongruously included among some glossy picture books of strange exotic birds and architecturally excellent houses in a hospital art library trolley that I was tidying up. The strangeness of its presence grabbed me, so I borrowed it and read my way to another sphere of liberating affirmation.

I love autobiographies, stories written by real people about themselves. It became an intentional reading preference because of a comment from an unexpected source on my wedding day. My hair stylist, busy creating an exotic style to go with my wedding head-gear said, "I read all the time, but mostly autobiographies and biographies. Why waste time on lives that didn't happen when real lives are so exciting". Novels tell about life, but no matter how well done, there is always that consciousness that "this didn't really happen". In autobiographies, reality is never destroyed. These people did exist. They did achieve or fail. They show us it is possible to live with awareness and authenticity and remind us that we can also make some mark in this world.

Autobiographies nudge us to change. The great Romanian historian of religion Mircea Eliade (1907-86) in his brilliant autobiography says

> Books can be loaded with dynamite, so that from an encounter with certain books, you can emerge either mutilated, or else ten times stronger than you believed you were. [119]

Change comes through observing how others have been caught up in the jigsaw of life and how they have made the pieces interlock. Some of their pieces fit our own life jigsaw and thus we learn from them.   Through autobiographies, unspoken thoughts long repressed within us may be authenticated by someone else's experience.   Our loftiest dreams and doubts are affirmed because someone else who also dreamed those doubts nurtured them into action. Frederick Buechner says about writing his autobiography:

> I do it ... in the hope of encouraging others to do the same - at least to look back over their lives, as I have looked back over mine, for certain themes and patterns and signals that are so easy to miss when you're caught up in the process of living them. ...If we keep our hearts and minds open as well as our ears...then I think we come to recognize, beyond all doubt, that, however faintly we may hear him, he is indeed speaking to us, and that, however little we may understand of it, his word to each of us is both recoverable and precious beyond telling. In that sense autobiography becomes a way of praying, and a book like this, if it matters at all, matters mostly as a call to prayer. [120]

The secret of being available to the nudges of doubt is not to read in one tradition only, but to investigate other theological paradigms for new nudges. If a new paradigm fits, wear it. Be suspicious though, if theories are too watertight or dogmatic, if faith must follow a pattern and if God is obedient, accommodating and - dull, like an English butler. If theological tidiness has not been your experience of life, trust your experience and don't be forced into second class citizenship for the sake of conformity. Hunt for writers who groan in your language. How-to religious books may have their fan clubs, like moths around the naked light, but some moths get burnt.

Nudges from doubt also come to us through relationships.   People are not just other ants on the anthill. They are fellow journeyers and, as such, also agents of divine persuasiveness. If we are people-persons, we must watch for nudges from others because, through people, God may have the best chance of luring us. Dan Wakefield (1932-) in his spiritual memoir says of a lecturer he encountered in college who helped him with his career decisions:

> I think of him now as one of those earthly "guardian angels" who suddenly appear in your life out of nowhere, offering a kind of confirming reassurance and appreciation, and serving as a guide to the next point in your journey. [121]

I experienced this when I first arrived in the United States from Australia to live for a period of time. After a few months of attending a large church, I realized I was not hearing the religious "words" from my past that I believed were crucial - salvation, sin, guilt, making a decision etc. I became disenchanted, even disdainful of the preaching. Yet the people were the most loving I had ever encountered in a church — accepting, gracious and warm. I was forced, therefore, to listen more closely to the preaching to discover their secret. This nudge pushed me to doubt my preconceived notions of holiness and correct God-talk and learn the path of love, action and tolerance. People's lives have become divine messages to me. If your doubts are needing attention at present, notice the people crossing your path. Perhaps one of them is the agent of grace for you.

I remember a preacher with a reputation for dullness. I did not anticipate much inspiration when he visited our church and my fears proved right. But, as if divine eyes metaphorically twinkled at my aloofness, a "pearl" was dropped unexpectedly in the midst of a laborious monologue, the missing link for my current question that could move me on in my pondering. For many in the congregation, nothing materialized, but my reluctant body was nudged to recognize the seed when it fell. Such experiences can also come from scripture if we are expectant and look for the three dimensional. Words can surprise us, standing out from the page in living shape, words previously read as two dimensional sentences. The sides, the shading, the edges, the "what ifs" of these words appear and we can smell, taste and feel the life that comes through them.

Life-changing conversations can be nudges as well. Such occur at random and often in most delightful ways. Chance comments lead us to rethink things, but we also need to be intentional in conversation, open for nudges. Conversations can be alive or dead. Many times I long to interject some very personal or controversial statement into a back-and-forth exchange of generalities, to test whether there is life in the dialogue, whether something more than anecdotes could survive. Sequential anecdotes merely masquerading as conversation remind me of the left-right-left neck action at tennis tournaments, continuing until someone calls "match". Meaning and relationship become expelled further with each new story, no matter how hard one wants to hold on to both.

In some conversations we play our part in a script, inserting our special opinions or prejudices on cue. To introduce an unprogrammed thought is like changing our lines on opening night. We are *expected* to play by the rules of social conversation, to avoid difficult issues and refrain from exposing too much of ourselves. Henry Thoreau said:

> We rarely meet a man who can tell us any news which he has not read in a newspaper, or been told by his neighbour; and, for the most part, the only difference between us and our fellow is that he has seen the newspaper, or been out to tea, and we have not. In proportion as our inward life fails, we go more constantly and desperately to the post office. You may depend on it that the poor fellow who walks away with the greatest number of letters proud of his extensive correspondence has not heard from himself this long while. [122]

For some, anecdotal conversation is deliberate. They cannot risk allowing their door to open, even a crack, leaving them vulnerable. They cannot trust themselves to others and thus they find few opportunities in a lifetime to share their faith story.

Intentional conversation allows for God to lure us to a new adventure. "Intentional" does not mean using communication skills techniques so that the other is conscious of being analysed. There is a place for that in counselling, but an intentional conversation is not a session where one leaves feeling exposed while the other has scarcely unbuttoned an overcoat; where one has been manipulated into admitting to being human but the other has not reciprocated. Intentional conversations require both parties to risk being vulnerable.

This is especially true in conversations about doubts. To believe the possibility of an intimate exchange, to share doubts and open the heart only to receive incredulous stares, feels like a turtle lying on its back - helpless, vulnerable, exposed and alone. This is part of the risk of believing that conversation can live. In such a situation, however, the loser is not the one risking humanness but the one afraid to risk. Jesus spent his life leaving himself vulnerable, to the crowds, the disciples, the government, the religious. Vulnerability led him to the cross, but also spawned a community who recognized his vulnerability as love.

So how can conversations become channels for nudges? When we are in the habit of recognizing divine activity in events in our own lives, this sensitivity continues into our conversations. We recognize nudges in similar concerns expressed by others, if we are used to recognizing nudges within our own experience. Many of our experiences with doubt also have the habit of sneaking into our conversations. Because they were born through our struggle, not through absorption of another's ideas, they belong to us and can transform a directionless conversation. Dialogue changes from listing of things to sharing of lives. When this happens, nudges have been recognized and both partners are lured into freedom. To experience such moments means opening our minds deliberately to the unexpected rather than repeating the past through our anecdotes.

Some time after this book was first published, a clergyperson wrote an editorial about it for a church paper. He dealt with only one point in the book, these last few paragraphs, pondering how much intentional conversation was happening in his church, in coffee times, committee meetings, bible studies. He noted that I had said both parties needed to be vulnerable, stating how hard it was in a big church to find places to be vulnerable in an accepting atmosphere. "Share with someone your doubts as well as your faith statements", he urged. A few months later, it emerged that the clergyperson himself had serious personal problems that he had been unable to share with anyone in his congregation. His plea for intentional conversation, safe places and the sharing of doubt was, in fact, his own plea for someone to listen non-judgmentally to *him*.

Doubts as nudges are also heard when we make time to listen, with minds cleared for long silences that allow doubts to whirl around freely. Short moments over set scripture passages or "thoughts for the day" do not necessarily create space for doubts to surface — *your* doubts may not fit into someone else's devotional solution. Doubts write their own agenda. As one doubt is solved, it leads to a new question, like clues in a murder mystery. This sequence of solutions and questions is part of the process, the work of faith.

For example, if a person changes her understanding about the meaning of the crucifixion or atonement, there will be many other beliefs that depend on the previous paradigm that will also have to be rethought. If a whole new paradigm for how to interpret scripture is adopted, the floodgates open. With over fifty different literary genres in scripture to decipher as to how they should be read, there is a lot of re-reading and re-thinking to be done! There will always be happenings and histrionics that prevent us from scheduling time to respond in honesty to our doubts, however. "When I get over this change in job situation, I will read some of the great Christian writers". "When I get a weekend off I will think about that". It is easy to be sidetracked. In fact, I think it is possible to live a whole life on sidetracks, sometimes on purpose. Many do this through busy work on church committees and community projects because busyness physically saves us from being alone with ourselves in silent moments that demand that we think.

Days come when, for the first time in months, there is nothing urgent - no papers to write, no meeting to attend. Hours stretch ahead, luring to potential adventure with a book, a journal to write, or some thinking about the nudges. But the desk needs clearing, pencils sharpened, shavings disposed of. The trash can is full. While emptying it, the weeds between the flagstones catch the eye. After the neighbourly chat, there is little point beginning without coffee. Then the mail comes. It is now three hours since the pencils were sharpened.

Many who long for solitude to work with doubts, and who would use it responsibly, cannot always *choose* such moments because of responsibilities and family commitments. Family people do not live in a world of monastic order. Doubts may accost us when the baby needs a bottle, the family waits for dinner, or another client is at the door. We don't have the luxury of discretionary time when we cannot be disturbed. It always strikes me as significant that so much good reflective writing comes from religious orders where personal time is more respected.

Theologian and missionary doctor Albert Schweitzer (1875-1965), when asked once how he got everything done, said that, for a long time, he put off what he wanted to do until he had an hour to spare. It was years before he realized he never found that hour and started using the minutes. I read this when my children were babies and there was never time to sit and think. I resented this loss of space until Schweitzer's words nudged me, not only to use the minutes, but also to accept that doubting and resolution is an ongoing process. We never arrive at "total knowledge" this side of the grave. Once one realizes there is no future moment of doubt-free certainty, one can better handle the frustration of not yet arriving.

Today's environment is not conducive to meditation or aloneness. The physical world competes for our attention, like a bunch of fans grabbing at your hand in a crowd. The information overload is part of the conspiracy, pushing us to absorb more information faster, yet we are falling behind because knowledge is produced faster than we can absorb even enough for our own needs. Solitude has become something for which to apologize. Going to a movie alone indicates one is friendless; eating alone in a restaurant requires explanation; lulls of silence in a conversation causes discomfort; and admitting one is not busy destroys our image. Noise is introduced to prevent silence. The church is not exempt here. Group prayer becomes uncomfortable if there are gaps of silence. Moments for meditation need background music. Silence seems to initiate frenetic action rather than reflection. Have we produced a religion of activity that has no room to reflect on such action?

It is not only finding alone time, but what to do in that aloneness. Reading may purely be cramming information to be regurgitated at the next party, a journalistic information-gathering process to facilitate social discourse. We scan newspapers for summaries of world issues so that we are equipped with information but which never "composts" into our own experiences. Trappist monk Thomas Merton (1915-68) wrote:

> How tragic it is that they who have nothing to express are continually expressing themselves, like nervous gunners, firing burst after burst of ammunition into the dark where there is no enemy. [123]

What transformation would happen if alone moments were spent developing our own awareness, using this as the content for future conversations? What if a decree allowed only original experience or thought in conversation, not borrowed quotes and theories? It would render some people speechless. It would change the face of religion. It would challenge us to think.

Some people do not accept career promotions because responsibility makes extra demands on them. In the same way, the invitation to greater richness of experience through listening to our doubts is also to take on work. This "road less travelled" demands discipline and there are few prepared to walk it. Doubters must reclaim for ourselves that verse "For the gate is narrow and the road is hard that leads to life and there are few who find it" (Matthew 7: 14)

This path can also mean alienation. Some label doubters as backsliders because we are not willing to accept simple answers and inconsistencies. A doubter friend of mine received a letter from an old friend. The doubter had written, explaining his emerging ideas about faith. Because these new thoughts threatened the belief foundations of the receiver and thus demanded work to understand the doubter's challenges, the response was, "If you want to keep writing such crazy ideas to me, and expect me to read them, I would rather you did not write again".

The search needs space. We can live fortressed in secure understandings and beliefs, or we can believe life is overflowing with new experiences that confront us, totally disorientate us and turn our lives around. A faith community needs to allow such people big paddocks to graze all over. Answers come when we go beyond where we have already walked and when we believe there is a solution if we search with faithfulness. Natalie Goldberg describes this same experience as a writer:

> Push yourself beyond when you think you are done with what you have to say. Go a little further. Sometimes when you think you are done, it is just the beginning. Probably that's why we decide we're done. It's getting too scary. We are touching down onto something real. It is beyond the point when you think you are done that often something strong comes out...I know it can be frightening and a real loss of control, but I promise you, you can go through to the other side and actually come out singing. You might cry a little before the singing, but that is OK. Just keep your hand moving as you are feeling. Often, as I write my best pieces, my heart is breaking. [124]

So many times in my own experience, there have been moments when the sun shone through and I wanted to bask in that moment. But there was so little time before another thought emerges to question. When I looked at others who seemed to sail along on a cloud of all knowing, I thought "Why am I so obsessed with who God is? Why can't I accept without question the teachings imposed on me?" But at those moments I reminded myself that doubts are an inner voice saying "You haven't seen anything yet!"

It takes so much to be a full human being that there are very few who have the enlightenment or the courage to pay the price. One has to abandon altogether the search for security and reach out to the risk of living with both arms. One has to embrace the world like a lover, and yet demand no easy return of love. One has to accept pain as a condition of existence. One has to court doubt and darkness as the cost of existence. One needs a will stubborn in conflict, but apt always to the total acceptance of living and dying. [125]

---

[105] Keller, *From a Broken Web*, 6

[106] Hugh Mackay, "The Joy of Doubting: that's no doubt about it" in *The Age* (Melbourne), 26.2.2000, B9

[107] Frank Schaeffer, *Crazy for God: how I grew up as one of the elect, helped found the religious right, and lived to take all (or almost all) of it back* (Philadelphia: Da Capo Press, 2007), 32

[108] Schaeffer, *Crazy for God*, 33

[109] Virginia Ramey Mollenkott, "Confronting Fundamentalism", in *Open Hands*, Fall 1993, 8

[110] Buechner, *The Sacred Journey*, 78

[111] Rex A. E. Hunt & John W. H. Smith, eds. *We Weren't Told: a Handbook of progressive Christianity* (Salem, OR: Polebridge Press, 2012)

[112] Goldberg, *Writing Down the Bones*, 14

[113] Malcolm Muggeridge, *Jesus Rediscovered* (Glasgow: Collins, 1969)

[114] Henry David Thoreau, *Walden* (New York & Toronto: Signet Classic New American Library, 1960), 77

[115] Dietrich Bonhoeffer, *Letters and Papers from Prison*, Eberhard Bethge, ed. (New York: Macmillan Publishing Co., 1979)

[116] Bamber Gascoyne, *The Christians* (New York: William Morrow & Co. Inc., 1977)

[117] Edward Schillebeeckx, *Jesus* (New York: Vintage Books, 1981)

[118] Hans Kung, *The Christian Challenge* (London: Collins, 1979)

[119] Mircea Eliade, *Autobiography* (San Francisco: Harper & Row, 1981).

[120] Buechner, *Now and Then*, 3

[121] Dan Wakefield, *Returning* (New York: Doubleday, 1988), 80

[122] Henry David Thoreau, *Walden and other Writings* (New York: Modern Library, 1937), 723-4

[123] Quoted in Cecil, Rieu & Wade, compilers, *The King's Son*, 31-2

[124] Goldberg, *Writing Down to the Bones*, 103

[125] Alice & Walden Howard, *Exploring the Road Less Travelled* (New York: Simon & Schuster, 1985), 21

Chapter 10.   Doubts and the Faith Community

To take risks is the safest thing for a Christian to do. The sturdiest
faith comes out of a struggle with doubt. One thing I know for sure: in
the business of living one must not live with certainties but with
visions, risks and passion. Visions: to see the future in hope and expect
the best of people and situations. Risks: to venture forth in faith and
not to count the cost. Passion: to feel with all one's heart, to show
emotion, to share one's deepest experiences. This is to be saved by
hope.

Charles Birch [126]

We have come a long way since the beginning of the book. We have
seen that faith is not simply a set of beliefs to be accepted as true; that doubt
is an essential part of faith; and that, if we take doubts seriously as an arena
of divine action, we will find ourselves reaching beyond who we already are.
As scientist Charles Birch points out, this introduces uncertainty as well as
certainty into our lives, but uncertainty and doubt are always the
consequences of risk and they form part of everyday living, whether we are
religious or not.

How then, if people are each on their own life journeys, responding to
their own experiences and doubts, is it possible to live together in a faith
community without tearing each other apart or forcing everyone to
conform? This is no new problem. More wars have been fought over this,
both inside churches and on battle fields, than any other issue. What do we
have in common? I believe the one unifying factor within any community
expression of faith is that great command to love - love God and love your
neighbour. It comes down to relationships rather than creeds.

This is the base on which we can work. Interpretation of doctrine
comes and goes, splitting families, communities and even individuals apart.
Belief systems rise and fall, causing wars and racial tensions. Religious
leaders claim exclusive revelations, then crumble because their feet are clay.
Scripture is used and misused as a weapon at the whim and bias of groups

and individuals. The one thing that can hold us together, even when we differ in theologies and experience, is a relationship of love. It is interesting that Jesus preached relationship rather than dogma. He rejected not only the Pharisees' attempt to corral every possibility into a law, but also many rules that focused on legality rather than love. If the lines from John's gospel attributed to Jesus, "I am the way, the *truth* and the life" (John 14: 6) could be interpreted in terms of relationship rather than dogma, these words could invite us to *be* on the journey with God, rather than condemning us for our doubts.

History has repeatedly shown that reverting to traditionalism or literalism does not solve problems of diversity of thought. No matter how carefully one tries to produce a hothouse of homogeneous believers, there is always the little boy who cries out, "He's naked". Homogeneity can only survive in a community if doubters are forced to leave, but such survival mentality leaves little room for novelty, for the suspicion that maybe "truth" is still to be found. Henri Nouwen said:

> When we are willing to detach ourselves from making our own limited experiences the criterion for our approach to others, then we will be able to see that history is greater than our history, experience is greater than our experience, and God is greater than our God. [127]

The funny part about debates about "true" doctrine is that we have never been able to "doctrinalise" the central concept of our religion - love. To put the adjective "true" before it, which is what we do with all other authoritative dogmas, throws it crazily into a category in our culture that is the opposite of rational thought. True love in all meanings of that phrase can only be described in terms of relationship. One can love chocolate, broccoli or movies, but "true love" conjures up an intensity that we only give to relationships. Love as a relationship cannot be captured in a definition but only described in the particularities of the thousands of experiences we call love.

In reality, we *do* tend to be grouped in denominations according to overarching doctrinal positions, but the majority of us who claim a denominational affiliation did not do so by a selective process of comparative study, but rather were *born* into a community and thus espoused its doctrinal umbrella. While we grew up accepting the dogma, it was the relationship with the church community that held us there or forced us to leave. When a community sees adherence to certain propositions as the "glue" that determines the community and affiliates is members, doubting Thomases may have no place. Like a possessive friendship, there are set rules and ways one must behave if one is to be in the fellowship. This is not love, but a power situation of one over the other.   The motto of the community may be "Love God and love the neighbour", but the subtitle specifies which description of God is to be the object of that love and how the neighbour must respond in order to be the recipient of the community's love.

I have just finished a conversation with a church leader about a small country church where literalist theology is being imposed on members. The lectionary is not used for preaching — a few powerful leaders simply choose the topics and bible verses for Sunday worship and give them to the designated lay preacher for that day. If the preacher moves beyond prescribed theology, according to those in power, he or she is not put on the preaching roster again. This is happening within a denomination noted for its inclusivity of theologies and openness to social justice, yet in this particular small church, a powerful few control what people hear and read. They have even refused to allow in their congregation the denomination's monthly magazine telling what churches across their state are doing, simply because this magazine might expose the congregation to "radical" or "liberal" ways of thinking which the church leadership see as non-Christian or evil. The person telling me this, rather than smuggling bibles into *China*, is currently smuggling issues of the church magazine into their pews.

This is not to say that communities of faith tied tightly together by strict doctrinal positions are not loving. In my experience, many people who have grown up in restrictive religious traditions *have* experienced loving community, both in families and in their church setting. Such communities often form strong bonds of solidarity because they feel under attack from the evils of the world outside their tradition. This solidarity makes it doubly hard for doubters, since a rejection of their childhood tradition may be interpreted also as a rejection of the people who nurtured them and, in fact, gave them the security in childhood that equipped them with tools of self-confidence to later face their doubts and challenge the tradition that mothered them! Doubters are forced to choose in such communities, when the hospitality of love plays second fiddle to conformity of doctrine.   One is not usually thrown out or ex-communicated, but pressured to believe, or be labelled a backslider.

Where a community sees their central glue as love and allows their experiences of loving God and neighbour to shape their theological reflection rather than humanly constructed doctrines, love becomes unconditional hospitality. Doctrinal uniformity is secondary (if not third or fourth) to hospitality. Hospitality is an attitude, a way of life. It is a willingness to create space so that people can find room to move, to grow, to be on their own life journey as well as the corporate journey. Hospitality allows a search for God without fear, without force to accept another's experience as the norm. Such hospitality allows gay, lesbian, transgender and bisexual people a safe place in our churches, women a place in our pulpits and people of other faiths a right to be heard and respected for their beliefs. Nouwen said:

> There are just as many ways to be a Christian as there are Christians, and it seems that more important than the imposition of any doctrine or idea is to offer people the place where they can reveal their great human potential to love, to give, and to create, and where they can find the affirmation that gives them the courage to continue their search without fear. Hospitality is to encourage each other to reflection which can lead to vision - but to their vision and not ours. [128]

Churches that find it impossible to realize that their truth is not the only truth cannot exhibit genuine hospitality. They may appear to be the most active in inviting people to try their fellowship and may also be fast growing congregations numbers-wise, but this is not the hospitality of which I speak. Hospitality is not demonstrated by how many come, but how long they stay and how much their staying depends on their willingness to conform.

So many people today list their major fear as loneliness and alienation. Such people will conform to anything purely to belong, to be wanted. The major draw card of gangs in our generation is that gang members have time for others in the group, make them feel wanted, give them a sense of belonging — things their families and birth communities have failed to do. For this acceptance, however, initiates have to obey the rules and carry out gang action, even if they doubt its ethics. A double-sided dose of fear holds such groups, church or gang, together — the fear of those in power that diversity may threaten their power base and challenge their own convictions and phobias; and the fear of those without power that their doubting of the rules may terminate their ability to belong.

Would Jesus have difficulty finding hospitality in churches today with his shockingly casual attitude to doctrinal integrity?   In Mark 9:38-42, the disciples complain to Jesus that a man was casting out demons in Jesus' name, yet he was not a follower — hadn't graduated from their seminary. Jesus' reaction was "Whoever is not against us is for us" and he goes on to condemn any of the disciples who would put a stumbling block before anyone — "It would be better for you if a great millstone were hung around your neck and you were thrown into the sea".   This story needs some examination because it illustrates many of the issues of doubt and a community.   This story is usually preached as a deterrent to those who venture to teach a theological idea contrary to the norm. Days of fear were generated for me as a doubter because of this passage.   It seemed that I was in considerable eternal trouble personally because of my internal questioning but, should that not be a sufficient deterrent to doubt, there was this added threat for those who taught "wrong" doctrine — having a millstone wrapped around my neck and thrown into the sea was a lesser punishment!

On closer examination, however, *who* might wear the millstone takes some interesting twists.   The disciples had tried to forbid this man casting out demons in Jesus' name because he was "not following us", not part of their group.   But Jesus said, "Do not stop him; for no one who does a deed of power in my name will be able soon after to speak evil of me.   Whoever is not against us is for us".   It's interesting how few times this awfully *inclusive* text is preached compared with that contrary text, "No one comes to the father but by me" (John 14: 6).   Virginia Mollenkott calls this the "supermarket approach" to the Bible, where teachers

> ....put into their cognitive shopping-carts whatever passages seem to suit
> their preconceptions and simply leave on the shelf those passages that
> seem less gratifying. [129]

The disciples were obviously bent out of shape because the other man seemed to be forming a branch church.   He was claiming miraculous powers in the name of Jesus and attracting a following without the disciples checking his credentials or even training and ordaining him.   How could they be sure he wasn't into wrong doctrine?   It was an authority issue for them — the man was operating without a ticket.

Jesus does not seem to understand the magnitude of the problem that someone was using his name as their authority for preaching and healing. He immediately equated this "deed of power" (casting out demons), which usually identified one as a charismatic leader, with the simple act of giving someone a glass of water. For Jesus, to love the neighbour was to show compassion for the other whether they needed water or exorcism. The disciples, however, would not have been fussing had the other man simply been giving drinks to the thirsty. Jesus was concerned instead with compassion, not correct doctrine. He was happy for a variety of workers, so long as they were not against his message of a coming reign of love and justice.

There is a second twist. Jesus does not continue to speak about the one "freelancing". He turns the conversation around to address the disciples and says, "If any of *you* put a stumbling block before one of these little ones who believe in me, it would be better for *you* if a great millstone were hung around your neck and *you* were thrown into the sea" (v 42, my italics). As if the millstone is not enough, he expands by instructing them to amputate feet, hands and eyes if these cause them to lead others astray. Thus, when the disciples wanted to claim special authority as those affiliated with Jesus, Jesus denied their exclusive claims and affirmed the equality of any who work in his name. He also broadened the nature of the tasks by relativising *all* roles - water-giving or exorcism - to the priority of love. As a triple whammy to those who wanted to control doctrines and office, Jesus warned that the inclination to heresy did not lie outside the gates but *within* their group. It was the disciples, not the one acting without authorization, that were at risk of punishment if they caused their followers to stumble.

Jesus closes this affirmation of diversity with the words "Be at peace with one another" (v.49). The issue about false doctrine was dissipated and love, inclusivity and tolerance become the glue for unity in diversity. In the Matthew reference to this episode, Jesus also talks about welcoming others and being welcomed in the name of Jesus. Hospitality and caring, not correct doctrine and right belief, are the reasons for any "reward". He says:

> Whoever welcomes you welcomes me, and whoever welcomes me welcomes the one who sent me. Whoever welcomes a prophet in the name of a prophet will receive a prophet's reward; and whoever welcomes a righteous person in the name of a righteous person will receive the reward of the righteous; and whoever gives even a cup of cold water to one of

> these little ones in the name of a disciple - truly I tell you, none of these
> will lose their reward (Matthew 10: 40)

This passage may not be the first one that springs mind for a sermon
on community, but it has many hints about such relationships. Jesus'
hospitality of love and inclusivity is a radical departure from what many
churches and communities are today. We are imprisoned in doctrinal
positions and traditional interpretations of God, lifestyle, morals and
salvation which we view as ultimate truth; and in structures of authority that
support these traditions, even though paradigm changes *have* been the
history of Christianity.

In 1977, the Uniting Church in Australia emerged as a new paradigm
from three previous paradigms when the Methodists, some Presbyterians
and the Congregationalists in Australia came into Union. While
recognizing their different heritages, the new *Basis of Union* document went
beyond all three. Part of the first paragraph reads:

> They [members of the Uniting Church in Australia] praise
> God for [God's] gifts of grace to each of them in years
> past; they acknowledge that none of them has
> responded to God's love with a full obedience; they
> look for a continuing renewal in which God will use
> their common worship, witness and service to set
> forth the word of salvation for all people. To this
> end they declare their readiness to go forward
> together in sole loyalty to Christ the living Head of
> the Church; they remain open to constant reform
> under his Word; and they seek a wider unity in the
> power of the Holy Spirit.

Some did not enter this union, unwilling to compromise their beliefs or
accept anyone else's version of the "truth". Others who entered Union had
little intention of changing — they simply saw Union as bringing more
people to their way of thinking. These people discovered, however, that
once they agreed to risk doctrinal "purity" as it were and pledge to work
with diversity, God introduced surprises that took them in new directions,
areas they did not always want to go. Some had to trample over their
stereotypes in order to see what they had not seen before, to learn the gift of
hospitality.

If hospitable love and compassion becomes the unity of our life together in community rather than allegiance to a set of doctrines, we can affirm that we are all on journeys and need to support and encourage each other at each point of those journeys.   As fellow journeyers, we can understand the other's experience of doubt, joy and frustration and show love and concern for that person.   A science student cannot answer the last minute questions of the commerce student at exam time, but there is a strong bond of unity in pre-exam suffering.   Each understands the tension, the apprehension, the exhaustion of the other and are together in the pain of the journey.

In the last paragraph, I added the word "compassion". Although I talked about love as the glue in the first edition of this book, love can sometimes become a slippery word as we use it for so many different acts and emotions. Compassion, however, conveys the same responsibility and attention to the other without becoming mired in romantic intoxication. If we think compassion-talk sounds light-weight for solving the problems of living in community, we have not scratched even the first layers of the word. Compassion does not mean feeling sorry for someone, or having pity, or decrying violence on our TV screens. The root meaning of compassion is "to suffer with" or the "endure something with another". Anyone who has sat with their child as he or she struggled for a final breath, or carried a mutilated body from a marketplace after a terrorist bomb, or seen the despair on an African mother's face as her baby frantically sucks an empty breast, knows that compassion surges up from within in response to such injustice and pain. Compassion is also an intentional act, the Golden Rule says, of identifying what gives pain to ourselves so that we refuse to impose such pain on another.   In the history of any religion, there have been moments of tremendous compassion, unimaginable cruelty and all points in between.   "We can either emphasize those aspects of our traditions, religious or secular, that speak of hatred, exclusion, and suspicion", religion scholar Karen Armstrong says, "or work with those that stress the interdependence and equality of all human beings. The choice is ours".[130]

Compassion demands that we respect each other, the central human desire according to Australian social commentator Hugh Mackay. Respect means to take others seriously, not overlooking or belittling them, something most political parties today need to hear. Respect withheld to an individual, group or nation can lead to violence, as we have seen when nations refuse to listen to the perspectives of another or refuse to consider how their actions might impoverish or disempower others. People denied respect can repeat the cycle by failing to respect those who come after them — oppressed nations become oppressors. The Puritans left England for religious freedom but killed Quakers on the Boston Common in America, refusing to give *them* religious freedom.

Compassion is about true listening. Caring enough to listen tells me that you care about who I am and what I think. Not really listening or "feeling with" the other —compassion — means that you do not hear what I am saying and signals that I am not worth listening to. True dialogue also means listening, not for an opening to argue, teach or correct, but with genuine hunger to learn from an equal. When we *do* talk, compassion does not condemn, judge or manipulate the conversation but invites further revelations. Each of our views might be couched in different language and doctrinal beliefs but our struggles as human beings are similar and we learn techniques for survival and flourishing from others.

We are also not really listening if we listen only through the filter of our particular beliefs and agenda. Bertrand Russell (1872-1970) wrote of the questions he had as a young man and how his doubts kept growing, yet he couldn't talk to anyone about them because they had their fixed ideas. He said:

> Through this time, I had been getting more and more out of sympathy with my people. I continued to agree with them in politics, but in nothing else. At first I sometimes tried to talk to them about things that I was considering, but they always laughed at me, and this caused me to hold my tongue. [131]

I remember speaking on doubt at a retreat and, over coffee afterwards, one person cornered me to ask "Do you believe in the virgin birth?" When I began, helpfully I thought, to dissect the various scholarship and thinking around this, he interrupted "No, do *you* believe in the virgin birth?" He wanted a "yes" or "no" answer with no discussion of what was meant by "virgin" or why this story is only in two of the Gospels and not the earliest, Mark, or the earlier writings of Paul. If I said "no", his beliefs were such that he could immediately dismiss anything I had said throughout the retreat, even though it might have caused some stirring in his heart and mind. According to Mackay:

> Listening is a form of therapy we can all offer each other, if we choose to. In fact, if I had to identify one way to make the world a better place, I'd say: Listen more attentively and sympathetically to each other. [132]

Compassionate listening leads to compassionate speaking. When a school mate said something mean to us as children, we chanted one of the earliest lies taught to us, "Sticks and stones may break by bones but words will never hurt me". Of *course* words hurt. Some people carry those hurts of early verbal abuse to their death bed. Do to others what you would have them do to you means speak to others as you would have others speak to you. Bullying is blossoming today, with the ability on Internet and Face book to trash other people without the deterrent of eye contact or physical presence, leading in some tragic cases to suicide. As for today's media, we are shaped by sound-bites and shock journalism that incite controversy, rather than nuanced arguments and fair presentation of issues, because controversy sells advertising and papers. I have been very frustrated to learn from moderate Muslim colleagues in Australia that their nuanced articles submitted to major newspapers about Muslims are often not published and, when phoned for a comment about a local issue involving Muslims, they are ignored in preference to someone who will make provocative or fanatic claims.

Compassion to the "other", whether someone within our faith community or someone from another religious faith, means opening ourselves to feel deeply with them, not in order to convert them but to learn with and from them. As the new Atheists claim, so much conflict and tragedy in the world has been caused by people defending their God and their truth yet really, to know only one religion or set of beliefs is to know *none*. It's like saying oranges are my favourite fruit when I haven't tasted any other. This has been the stance of exclusivist traditions for centuries, important enough to erect fences, conduct heresy trials, murder unbelievers or pronounce all other ideas false. Exclusivist attitudes have been passed on with breast-milk. When I was growing up, Protestants thought all Catholics were going to hell and Catholics thought the same about Protestants. As for other religions, we were filled with stories at Sunday School of missionaries going to "dark" places to bring "light" to "pagan" children. Fortunately today, more people see truth in other religions as paths to the Divine, allowing us the freedom to show interest in what people from different religions — our school teachers, doctors, workmates and friends — actually think.

When hospitality and compassion are central to communities rather than doctrinal uniformity, new metaphors for "church" emerge. The church is a base camp where shelter and provisions provide nurture and nourishment for mountain climbers. The survival of the climber depends on the presence and support of the base camp. There can be many different climbers, different techniques, different equipment, different peaks, yet all use that base camp for strength, provisions and shelter. A church is like a good marriage. The individuals in the partnership do not have to be on the same personal journey or have the same responsibilities or follow the same career. Each appoints the other guardian of their solitude as well as their togetherness and gives permission for the pursuit of uniqueness and individuality. At the same time, their life *together* nourishes and strengthens each for their respective ways.

Sharing of doubts is something church communities have not handled well and we have already seen why in our discussion of negative attitudes to doubt. It is a problem for both clergy and laity. The current hang-ups are immense, as are the repercussions. However, if the church community began to take doubt seriously as a catalyst for growth, hospitality could result. Providing hospitality for the sharing of doubts as well as triumphs would be the greatest step a church community could take towards unity and unconditional love.

To imagine what such communities could be like, we can borrow from the scientific community the image of a scientific conference. Such conferences provide opportunity for scientists in similar fields to share their research. The aim of most conferences is not only to present great discoveries but also to report on current progress. A paper may simply state that a particular drug has not worked after years of testing; another may solve only a fraction of a puzzle; another may report a breakthrough in method which has repercussions somewhere else; and another may admit no progress at all with a certain procedure.

There is no fear of reporting failure or lack of progress because these experiences are part of the scientific journey. People don't usually cover up results to impress others, although this has happened at times. Names are not struck off registers, ridiculed or shamed because they have not yet solved their equation. Instead, colleagues listen and learn from others' experiences, offer feedback from their own experiences, make suggestions of potential new avenues and question false assumptions. The conference meets to encourage each other, to assure each other the pursuit is worthwhile and to share new ideas which benefit all.

The glue that holds scientific conferences together, despite diversity, is respect for each other's struggles and successes and a common commitment to the scientific process. As we have seen in the discussion on scientific paradigm changes, theories and laws are not eternal truths but "frameworks" of understanding agreed upon, open to challenge should they be shown inadequate. Scientists constantly test scientific "doctrines" against experience through experiment, rather than treating theory or doctrine as infallible and subordinating new results to the theory. It is the commitment to each other, a trust in the community and its purpose, that binds. Of course, there are always the politics of obtaining grants and the possibility of shady research, as in any endeavour, but the comparison I am making is with the attitude to doubt and challenge.

In the same way, a hospitable church community's glue is the compassionate commitment to each other as we work on our own particular faith journey. A church community based primarily on adherence to a set of beliefs is like a scientific conference that accepts research papers only if they keep within certain "universal truths" e.g. belief that the earth is flat. To stay in such a scientific community, one must force one's results to fit this or give lip service to the theories, keeping one's own conclusions secret.

In a community where hospitality rather than conformity reigns, major doubts as roadblocks can be owned *during* the problem, not just in retrospect when solutions have come. A clergyperson can stand up and say, "All is lousy at this present moment. I cannot be bothered wrestling with this belief system anymore. It's not worth the effort, and I'm not sure God is real anyway". Such a testimony will not be taken as weakness or ignorance but as part of the process on the way. People will not be judged as novices who have not arrived because none of us know a point of arrival. We don't have final conclusions, but rather meet God in the process. Those communities who emphasize "before and after" scenarios only encourage testimonies in retrospect. A year from now one can mention a "low" time, but only when "full assurance" has been recovered.

Let us bring back into our communities the dynamics of fellow searchers who love each other regardless of diversity of theology. Let us listen again to the psalmists who raged at God and stomped, doubting loudly, through their journeys. Let us be refreshed and challenged by testimonies of saints who call on God and hear nothing in return, yet cling on, hoping for light in darkness. While to the outer world Mother Teresa was the poster child for great faith, at the same time she was enduring years of desolation and doubt. In a letter she addressed to Jesus at the request of her confessor in 1959, she said:

> In my heart there is no faith — no love — no trust — there is so much pain — the pain of longing, the pain of not being wanted — I want God with all the powers of my soul — and yet there between us — there is terrible separation. — I don't pray any longer — my soul is not one with you.[133]

Let us create a ethos in our churches and community groups where the most "spiritual" among us can stand up and talk about their arid faith without feeling demoted or exposed, but rather loved and encouraged. Let us not pray *for* them but *with* them, sharing the excitement of where their doubts will take them for the benefit of all.

When doubt is not allowed to surface in a church, the charade goes on. I had a recurring horror image in church as a child. I don't know where it originated - a comic strip, or perhaps a minister posed the possibility from the pulpit. I imagined that one day, becoming so angry with our doubt and hypocrisy, God superimposed a visible, cartoon word balloon above each head in church, spelling out exactly what each was thinking and what shams we all were. We can be actors par excellence if we feel it necessary for survival in an inhospitable community. We know the right words to inject in prayers. We know humble phrases that disguise power-hungry motives in committees. We can mouth acceptable tales of our journey without telling it from the heart and exposing feet stuck firmly in mud. There is no way our spirituality can be measured, no lie detectors as we proclaim what the Lord is doing for us, and God has never resorted to writing our spiritual score in permanent ink on our foreheads.

Honest doubt will best begin to be recognized as creative when somcone well-respected in the community is willing to cry "naked" first. This is the catch. Most of us stuck in inhospitable communities do not want to tarnish our image because we know inhospitable human nature revels in another's demise or exposure. While we are quick to say that the church is a place of sinners, we do not want it to be *that* obvious!

I sat in many prayer meetings, bible studies and fellowship groups, longing to ask questions that tore me apart, but I did not have the courage to expose my weaknesses when such seeming confidence surrounded me. Finally I came to realize that, if there were better answers, I should go to where answers were formulated - in theological departments. I told some friends I was registering for a degree in the university religion department. They assured me I would lose my faith. Even this is indicative of the problem! Such a reaction suggested that many had already moved from inhospitable communities into college studies looking for answers but, rather than such communities being interested in what they were learning, they tried to frighten folk from leaving the fold. As some said, I did lose something - my too-small belief systems — but my *faith* in something grasped me tighter through it all.

What such study did for me was to allow me to believe in and trust my own experience. I realized that fear of something new held inhospitable communities together. Now, with some religious studies under my belt, I could speak my doubts, equipped with my own "authority" of knowledge. I could raise questions, even if I did not know all the answers, knowing that the *questions* were legitimate to ask and had been raised by theologians across the centuries. It comes back to the power of "authority" as the way to silence those who doubt. I began to make it my mission, in small groups, committee meetings and in general conversation, to verbalize the doubts I suspected others may also be concealing. Without fail, flood gates opened and others finally felt at liberty to admit similar experiences. This leads me to think that the majority of us, though we might seem to have it all together on the surface, are struggling underneath. We are acting in a play, wearing masks over the darker thoughts of our life.

The issue of hospitality is one for both clergy and lay people. In the enthusiasm and idealism of youth, clergy people pledge themselves to the church. Yet the piece of paper that declares one a Minister of the Word does not also promise that one will never doubt. Experiences come that challenge established belief systems; new theologies question older norms; and, like everyone else, there are times when clergy feel remote from God, stumbling in bleak places. But few churches have ways to accommodate this in their clergy. Lack of hospitality prevents the pastor feeling safe or loved enough to expose himself or herself in any way.

Clergy are supposed to be the people with the answers. Even if laity claim they no longer see the clergy in this way, in truth they do. For any of us who has struggled with doubt, we know that struggle can go on for years. Is it different for clergy? Do we assume the struggle does not happen to them and may be continual? And where can clergy go when they have a faith crisis? They can talk to colleagues, but these peers are also those who influence career moves. They can talk to members of their congregations but thus open themselves to vulnerability if a hospitable climate turns stormy. Without hospitality, they have to stay in the pulpit, tearing apart inside. They are condemned to weep alone at night to that elusive God who on Sundays they so joyously and confidently proclaim.

Have you ever heard a priest say from the pulpit, "I'm having trouble with my beliefs; please bear with me"? You won't, unless safe hospitality has been declared for clergy and laity alike in the church. Should the pastor confess doubts without this guarantee of support, the pastor loses the position of strength created by the false expectations of the congregation (and also some acquiescence to this image on the pastor's part). And so the cycle goes on. This is the single most crucial factor in this whole issue. Only if we can share our doubts without recrimination can we all grow and mature, benefiting from each others' wisdom and experiences, clergy and lay alike.

The clergy problem cannot be blamed only on laity who do not allow them to be vulnerable. Clergypersons have also created the problem for themselves by allowing the "saint of God" image to develop or persist. While they may not verbalize this image, many do not refute it if it emerges, or verbally refute it while still enjoying its benefits. Sometimes this image is used as a mask, deterring closeness with people who may see their uncertainties. Clergy people in pastoral care may encourage the parishioner to be vulnerable but never reciprocate any feelings in common. When a clergyperson's doubts are in conflict with the confessional position one is ordained to represent, it also puts a double noose around the neck that can be jerked from either direction - pew or institution.

One argument put forward by clergy with whom I have talked about why doubts cannot be preached from the pulpit is that they would unsettle people who have not faced those particular questions. That argument is difficult for me to buy. The poor pew-sitters are left in a false security, to be exposed to the issues later in crisis, rather than in safe sanctuary in the community of believers where questions can be raised and opportunities given to work through the doubts together. When doubts surface in situations of hostility - a challenge from a friend who bulldozes one's spiritual foundations or when a death makes God seem unfair - the doubter struggles, unaware the pastor has also faced similar personal crises. Or, if a lay person in the pew is currently struggling in a dark place and the clergyperson always preaches joy and light and certainty, the hearer is doubly doomed and left condemned for their doubt.

Karen Armstrong, in her autobiography *The Spiral Staircase: a Memoir,* tells of her anger when she could finally stand back from the Roman Catholic Church and the convent she joined for many years and realize how the authorities told people what to believe and punished them if they didn't. Armstrong recalls a scene in the convent when she questioned the historicity of the resurrection and a senior sister agreed with her but added "but please don't tell the others". Armstrong says:

> I was convinced that I had not been alone in my doubts; there must be hundreds – thousands – of Christians who suppressed similar misgivings, stamped on their rebellious thoughts, and felt all the while a sinking loss of intellectual and personal integrity. These people must be crippling their minds as I had done by confining them within an untenable doctrinal system. [134]

So many times as a teenager, I longed that my pastor would allow some doubt to creep into a sermon so I did not feel so alone. Years later, when I was well into my theological studies, I worked with that pastor on a committee. He was asking about the classes I was taking and somehow the conversation came to church doctrines. He moved closer and said, "You know, I have always had trouble believing in the virgin birth and a bodily resurrection". My heart chilled because I could remember many Sundays when I had listened to him read those stories and preach on them with not a hint that the stories could be taken any way but literally. Each year I hoped I would hear an inkling of doubt over the Christmas or Easter stories, but each year I was condemned anew for my "problem" when no challenges were made to these stories. Oh for a minister to say from the pulpit, "This is a doctrine I doubt. I continue to struggle, just as I know many of you struggle with it and others. I would love to discuss this with some of you in a small group sometime". What a comfort that would be for so many. It opens the possibility of hospitality where all can believe that their membership depends on love for each other, not how neatly packaged our belief systems are and how well we believe them.

Some churches boast such hospitable structures - study groups, support groups, education opportunities - but these need to be examined carefully. Do they really create a safe space for people to share their most inward concerns, or do unspoken ground rules merely create an antechamber where one confesses only "acceptable" doubts. I may be willing to share the struggles I know are common experiences for all of us - anger, hurt, insensitivity - since they merely demonstrate that I am human. But will I also share the things that do not appear so universal? Would I be willing to say I can't believe, even though I still go through the motions? Would I be willing to say that, after twenty-five years of service in the church, I wonder if it is actually where God is found? Would I be willing to say that prayer feels like shouting into the wind? Or are these too honest for the low-risk confessionals of the average group?

Why is it that someone who is honest and straightforward in other areas of life feels so bound to silence about what is inside them? It is the nature of the faith that has often been sold to us, faith as a cumulative progression from conversion to saintliness, rather than the crazy, erratic path of a moth around a light bulb. Just a few months ago in a class I taught, someone quoted back to me something I had said a number of years earlier in another class. He had clung on to it because I had claimed that there was such a thing as "honest doubt". That moment had been the first time that person, in his seventies, had been given permission to admit his dark night of the soul within. He had been a leading lay person in the church all his life but, because of his longevity as a saint of the church, he had lost his ability to cry out "he's naked" for fear of rejection by the mob. On the other hand, Frederick Buechner described one of his courageous theology lecturers thus:

> "Every morning when you wake up", [the lecturer] would say, "before you reaffirm your faith in the majesty of a loving God, before you say I believe for another day, read the Daily News with its record of the latest crimes and tragedies of mankind and then see if you can honestly say it again". He was a fool in the sense that he didn't or couldn't or wouldn't resolve, intellectualize, evade, the tensions of his faith but lived those tensions out, torn almost in two by them at times. [135]

Creating hospitality begins with us enabling others to talk about the doubts of their hearts. It is to confront when real issues are not being allowed expression. It is to call a halt in discussions when third-person language never becomes first-person, or anecdotes never give way to deeper personal experience. It is to challenge when hard questions are dismissed with pious words or inadequate scripture. It is to be the little boy, prepared to be the fool that raises the question others are afraid to ask; that risks one's own place if it helps free the tongues of others. Such people are

> ...totally free to be. They are not burdened by any need to hide. They do not have to construct new lies to hide old ones. They need waste no effort covering tracks and maintaining disguises...By their openness, people dedicated to the truth live in the open, and through the exercise of their courage to live in the open, they become free from fear. [136]

Hospitality is an act of love. Jesus reduced all the commandments to that profound statement, "Love God and love your neighbour" (Matthew 22: 37-9). It is to this statement I return in my journey over and over again. When doctrines divide, when experiences clash, when ideologies roar at each other, all arguments are ineffective. Faith is expressed in unconditional love, love regardless of the cost, the circumstances, the conflict, the courage level. It means to love despite differences and this means folk outside our church community as well as inside. This book is not only about the doubts of church people who feel outcasts inwardly, if not also outwardly, but also for those who have left the church, disillusioned by traditional doctrines and silenced in their questioning, but who are still on the journey because they cannot give up.

To love one another unconditionally is the most blatant statement of transcending power we can make in today's world. When all other love offered is conditional, unconditional love shouts as clearly as a loon's call across a still Minnesota lake at midnight. It is so rare for people to be truly concerned today for another person's nurture, regardless of what they believe. To love in this way creates a sense of wonder, of disbelief, of amazement that forces the question "why"? Our lives are so geared to the constant impact of plastic happiness that the church can become just another shopping centre with panaceas for all our woes. What miracles happen when, for once, we are offered "true love" instead - caring, support, compassion, affirmation and hospitality with no strings attached.

"Nurture" means to nourish and nourishment should produce healthy growth. This is what true love seeks while protecting the uniqueness of the individual nourished. But nurture has another dimension in our culture. It means "bringing up or raising" in the sense of raising a child. This image is helpful or terrifying, depending on our childhood experiences. There are many church communities who see nurture as child-raising, the imposition of parental standards, beliefs and faith expectations on the child with threats and punishment to enlist conformity. This is not unconditional nurture.

To love unconditionally, to allow a loved one to tread a faith path different from our own, is scary. Scary, in that, like parents who want their children to be happy, we find it difficult to believe others may need a tradition different from ours. It is also frightening if our belief system depends on rewards or punishment for accepting "true doctrine". We fear our loved one will not discover the correct formula for salvation. The bravest thing parents can ever do is allow a child to follow a path other than their own and to love them unconditionally anyway. This is what we must learn to do within the church.

Such love and compassion is work — it is not just "feeling". It transcends desire and becomes action. To love is an act of will. Jesus' words "Love God and love your neighbour" summarize faith in community. To love God means that each is on a journey of doubt, faith and beliefs in the company of others on journeys who serve as carriers of God's nudges for us, affecting us and being affected by us. The more we love that which we call God, the more we realize that to love God is also to love our neighbour. Such is the interconnectedness of life.

---

[126] Birch, *Regaining Compassion*, 39

[127] Henri Nouwen, *Reaching Out* (New York: Doubleday. 1966), 76

[128] Nouwen, *Reaching Out*, 62

[129] Mollenkott, *"Confronting Fundamentalism"*, 8

[130] Karen Armstrong, *Twelve Steps to a Compassionate Life* (New York: Alfred A. Knopf, 2011), 22

[131] Bertrand Russell, *The Autobiography of Bertrand Russell* (Boston: Little, Brown and Company, 1967), 52

[132] Hugh Mackay, *What makes us Tick: the ten desires that drive us* (Sydney: Hachette Australia, 2010), 31

[133] Mother Teresa, *Come be my Light*, 193

[134] Armstrong, *The Spiral Staircase*, 261

[135] Buechner, *Now and Then*, 16-17

[136] Peck, *The Road Less Travelled*, 63

Chapter 11.   Have We Progressed at All?

For years I had told myself
that black was white and white black;
that the so-called 'proofs' for God's existence
had truly convinced me,
that I might not be feeling happy,
but that I really was happy
because I was doing God's will ...
I had deliberately told myself lies
and stamped hard on my mind
whenever it had reached out towards the truth.
As a result, I had warped
and incapacitated my mental powers.
From now on, I must be scrupulous
about telling the truth,
especially to myself.

Karen Armstrong [137]

Let me tell you a parable. Once upon a time, the gods gave a stream to the people telling them that, if they drank, they would find peace and happiness. The people drank and then gathered to share their experiences. They told the next village and others came to drink. The community grew. Some were appointed to build steps down to the stream, to help with foot traffic and roster each individual's time at the stream. One man took charge (for the good of the whole, of course) and gathered a group around him to study why people felt good after drinking, how the water came to be there and what was the best way to drink. Only the chosen could be in this discussion — and no women, for some reason. The group soon argued about *true* meanings and formed different camps. The dominant camp pooh-poohed all other stories and began to regulate who was eligible to drink, according to correct belief and purity of heart and body. They also declared that they could drink on behalf of those *not* eligible. Trouble brewed between strict letter-of-the-lawyers and pragmatic compassionates, the former regularly blocking the steps against the latter, often with violence. Of course, claims from passing travellers of similar streams in *other* places were dismissed as false or inferior.

After a long time, the old people began to talk, out of earshot of leaders, about when the gods first gave them the stream. Some even looked into a dusty file in the archives recording the event. They discovered, to their surprise, that, in the beginning, *everyone* could drink freely and equally by divine order and that the rules and explanations constructed over time were not in the file. They challenged the leaders — to no avail or with limited concessions granted. Some simply trudged further upstream where the banks were not patrolled and knelt to drink together, passing cups of water to the too young or too old. Downstream, their relatives continued to take turns on the steps and obey the rules. As Jesus said after he told a parable, "Those that have ears to hear, let them hear".

To this point, the content of this book has not significantly changed from the original edition as it is still relevant for peoples' experiences in so many churches. Doubts about the divinity of Jesus, the existence of God, virgin birth, resurrection and "truth" in other religions are still ignored, suppressed or dismissed because they challenge an inspired Bible or infallible Church. What many people in church pews do not know, however, is that these questions have been the diet of discussion in theological halls for centuries. People who challenge traditional answers are not being heretical or radical — they are simply bringing these discussions into earshot of the rest of us and this has happened to a much greater degree since this book was first published.

As already mentioned, biblical criticism, a method of interpretation of scripture that addresses such questions, emerged and developed in the eighteenth and nineteenth centuries and is commonplace in scholarly circles today yet, until lately, its findings have rarely reached the pews. Biblical criticism asks questions of the biblical text rather than simply taking first century words at twenty-first century face value. It asks historical questions e.g. what was going on at the time of writing that would influence the way the stories were told; how did people in Jesus' time evaluate his miracles when others were also performing miracles? It also asks canonical questions i.e. why were some gospels included in our New Testament canon and not others (for example, the Gospel of Thomas) and what was happening in fourth century church politics when the final selection of books for the Bible was made? It asks social questions - how did the subordinate status of women in Hebrew society and the Greco-Roman world influence the way women are portrayed in the Bible?

Biblical criticism also asks textual questions because, prior to the printing press, every word had to be *hand-copied* multiple times to distribute copies of the Bible and we don't even have any original documents, only copies from centuries after the events. In fact, some biblical manuscripts discovered in the Dead Sea Scrolls of Qumran and the Nag Hammadi library in Egypt in the 1940's are *earlier* manuscripts than those used in the King James Version published in 1611 and show variations in wording. This reflects not just copying errors but that copiers were authors themselves with a point of view to add. As an example, the King James Version records Matthew 5:22 as "Everyone who is angry with his brother *without a cause* shall be liable to judgment", but an earlier copy of Matthew found in the 1940's does not have "without a cause". Obviously, an interpreter along the way softened the verse, giving some latitude as to when one could legitimately get angry. Such textual changes are only problematic if we claim we have God's dictated words and an original script.

Biblical criticism also asks questions about changes in meaning of words over the centuries as this can lead to misinterpretation. It asks about the genre of various biblical writings — whether they were intended to be read as literal records, narrative, parables, stories, liturgy or sayings. It asks whether biblical books were originally single-authored documents or compilations by later authors from various sources, some of which are no longer in existence. Biblical criticism shows us that the Bible cannot just be read as something unaffected by human knowledge, human error, culture and circumstance, to be applied as is to twenty-first century life as if nothing has ever changed.

Those who object to this should think about other aspects of life. Is there any area — medicine, social structures, technology or cosmology — where we happily prefer first century conclusions to twenty-first century knowledge? Of course, such objectors would argue that the Bible is different because it is the *inspired* word of God and thus everything must be taken as "written by" or "approved by" God as models for living, but what does this mean? Today we would reject as a family model the story of Jephthah (Judges 11) who offered a bribe to God in exchange for military victory. God did not refuse the bribe, even though it was to sacrifice whomever greeted Jephthah first on his victorious return. As a result, Jephthah tied his young daughter to an altar, burning her as a thank-you to God. And, if you think Old Testament values were transformed by New Testament values, Jephthah was listed in the letter to the Hebrews as a great man of faith (Hebrews 11: 32) and slavery was never condemned by Jesus or Paul. The problem with literal biblical interpretation or the assumption that biblical commands must apply without critique in any century or culture is that it is always *selective*. People choose as dogma the bits that work for their agenda — for example, women having to keep silent in church — and simply ignore other problematic passages.

If, instead, we approach the Bible as the story of God's Spirit at work in certain communities in the ancient world, the same Spirit promised to be at work in communities writing new stories, in what way are the stories recorded in the end of the Acts of the Apostles more "inspired" than the stories that happened a month later, a year later or two thousand years later? When the Hebrew scriptures spoke of prophets being "inspired" by God, they did not mean overtaken by some divine power and ceasing to be human. They were well in control of their thoughts and actions and expressed what they wanted to say in accordance with their knowledge at that time. To argue that the Bible is inerrant because the writers were inspired is also problematic as we do not know who many of the individual writers *were* and some books had many writers and much editing. If God planned an inerrant book, why didn't Jesus spend less time talking and more time getting a divine dictation down on paper?

A more useful approach is to let the Bible define itself. The word translated as "inspired" occurs only once in the Bible to describe scripture (11 Timothy 3: 16) which was the Hebrew sacred texts, not all the gospels and letters as we have them today. The recipient of this letter is warned against false teaching and urged to "continue in what you have learned and firmly believed, knowing from whom you learned it". The writer says "All scripture is inspired by God and is useful for teaching, for reproof, for correction, and for training in righteousness, so that everyone who belongs to God may be proficient, equipped for every good work". We know that the Hebrew scriptures were open to interpretation and did not contain rules for all situations - that was why commentaries on the Torah were written and much debated. According to this verse, scripture is to be studied as a useful guide to faith but the reader must use his own mind to interpret it, not be led astray by interpretations of others — hardly a plea for a single dogmatic reading.

Inspired or "God-breathed" describes *all* humanity, according to the Genesis story. God breathed the divine breath or Spirit into all at creation and Jesus promised his disciples that this Spirit in him would continue with them, guiding them into all truth (John 16: 13). *We* are all therefore inspired, not just those unknown folk who compiled the early writings. The Spirit was in those who recorded the stories, in those communities who preserved, shaped and transmitted them; in those who shaped a canon and those who continue to interpret scripture, clergy and lay, including those who *challenge* interpretations that no longer work. Do we thus claim to be infallible or inerrant? No!

To claim the Bible is inspired by God is to affirm it as a human record of people, conscious of God's Spirit with them, who offer their stories and experiences as a guide for us to write *our* own stories of encountering that Spirit. Since the Bible is our source about Jesus, it has received special status in the church, but it is not the final story nor is it immune to critique in new circumstances. These writings provide a foundation on which we can build beliefs and world-views for new situations, not an infallible textbook of scientific, cosmological and theological laws. The latter actually negates the Bible and its promise that the Spirit is still working in our midst, bringing more light and truth to every generation. By distinguishing between the *words* of scripture and the *Word* or Spirit we encounter in scripture, we are freed from literal interpretations binding us to dogmas of a previous age.

In 1860, a group of well-known Anglican scholars from Oxford and Cambridge published *Essays and Reviews,* a collection that challenged many church beliefs set in stone and in particular, literal readings of the Bible. [138] Charles Darwin's (1809-82) *The Origin of Species by means of Natural Selection* had been published the previous year and some of these essays by scholars embraced the new science, urging the reading of the Genesis creation story as a Hebrew myth rather than literal truth. Using biblical criticism, they argued that the Bible should be

> ... interpreted like other books, with attention to the character of its authors, and the prevailing state of civilization and knowledge, with allowances for peculiarities, style and language, and modes of thought and figures of speech. [139]

These essays were immensely popular to the horror of the Church of England hierarchy. The writers were brought before church courts and some were charged — mathematician and Anglican priest Baden Powell (1796-1860), father of the founder of scouting, died before his trial. The others lived under a cloud as the powers that be did everything they could to discredit the book.

The message was out in the public, however, and many people felt validated about questioning scripture. The aunt of Darwin's wife had read around biblical criticism and also the emerging scientific discussions. Like the essayists, this did not perturb her as she did not need the Bible to be "dropped from heaven" in order to find in it

> ...all my heart wants, without believing that every word is inspired ... What puzzles me too much, or appears contradictory, I lay to the faults of the many hands through which it reaches me, and still clasp it to my heart as a divine book, however it may have been perverted by the perverse. [140]

Darwin, on the other hand, dealt in evidences. One of his biographers tells of a dream Darwin had that one day a historical manuscript would be discovered in Pompeii that "confirmed in the most striking manner all that was written in the Gospels" and proved a supernatural event had taken place. He was, at the time, reading Edward Bulwer-Lytton's novel *Last Days of Pompeii* about a secret Christian group in Pompeii and the possibility that some of their documents might be found dating from the catastrophe in 79 CE. In Darwin's time, Pompeii was still buried under rubble. [141]

In parallel with biblical criticism came "historical Jesus" research, the quest to uncover the "real" Jesus from layers of theological and cultural embellishment over the centuries. Scholars as far back as Hermann Reimarus (1694-1768) were asking to what extent the Christ of Christianity resembled the original Jewish Jesus and his mission. Albert Schweitzer summarized Jesus research in his 1906 book *The Quest for the Historical Jesus*, which was very threatening to those who did not want these questions to be asked. Schweitzer said:

> The satisfaction which I could not help feeling at having solved so many historical riddles about the existence of Jesus, was accompanied by the painful consciousness that this new knowledge in the realm of history would mean unrest and difficulty for Christian piety. I comforted myself,

however, with the words of St. Paul's which has been familiar to me from childhood: "We can do nothing against the truth, but for the truth" (2 Cor. 13: 8). [142]

Thus biblical criticism and historical Jesus research have been alive and well for over a century in theological schools that train clergy for our churches, but rarely have they been shared with laity because they ask awkward questions of outdated doctrines and church "tradition". Lay people have been kept in the dark with their doubts unanswered. In the turbulent sixties, however, many trickles of challenge became a flood. Vatican II shook the Roman Catholic world by opening the windows for some fresh, contemporary air; Liberation theology challenged those with power over oppressed peoples; and the little book *Honest to God* by John T. Robinson launched a theological revolution. Bishop Robinson did not say something entirely new — he was influenced by two mentors, Paul Tillich and Dietrich Bonhoeffer. However, his book was written, as an Anglican bishop, for the *public*, using biblical criticism tools and it hit the open marketplace like a bomb, becoming an immediate best-seller. This book freed many to ask their questions openly but, for others, it became the symbol of all that needed to be opposed and silenced. I was at university at the time and, while the Student Christian Movement devoured the writings of Robinson and others, the Evangelical Union of which I was a member felt it their mission to stamp out all such heresy. It would take more than a decade before I was privy to such writing!

Anglican Bishop Jack Spong, a fellow bishop in the Anglican communion, absorbed Robinson's words and has become a major international figure in what has become known as Progressive Christianity. When I first wrote my book on doubt, it was rejected by a number of publishers as a bit dangerous, but times are "a'changing" as the song says and, by the time my book finally came out in 1995, Spong had published controversial books on human sexuality, rescuing the Bible from fundamentalism, the virgin birth and the resurrection. [143] These were written, not for colleagues, but for thinking laity, as Robinson had done, whom Spong calls "church alumni" — people who have left the church, frustrated at its inability to address their doubts, or who sit uneasily in pews, stirring a little and hoping that, one day, their churches will be open to contemporary questions.

At the same time as Spong's books were appearing, Professor Marcus Borg's book *Meeting Jesus again for the First Time* captured the public marketplace, offering contemporary Jesus research to the laity. Borg is a member of the Jesus Seminar, begun by distinguished American New Testament scholar Robert Funk (1926-2005) in 1985. Funk gathered a group of significant New Testament scholars together as the Westar Institute with the mission to report a scholarly consensus on the historical authenticity of the sayings and events attributed to Jesus in the gospels. From this, profiles of Jesus have been drawn up by different scholars in the group. The Seminar continues its work on many questions and publishes its results through Polebridge Press. Although this type of research is also being done in universities and the Seminar people have university posts, the aim of the Jesus Seminar has been to write for the public rather than the closed halls of academia. They believe that lay people need to know the questions being asked and the answers formulated. Biblical scholar John Dominic Crossan (1934-) is a founding member of the Jesus Seminar and his work on discovering who Jesus was *within* his Jewish and Greco-Roman context has opened up a world of new understanding about Jesus' challenge to imperial Rome.

On the other side of the Atlantic, Richard Holloway, the Anglican Bishop of Edinburgh and head of the Scottish Episcopal Church, has struggled with his doubts about God and the teachings of the institutional church to which he belonged, a church that continued to enforce rules taken from biblical texts, regardless of the contemporary context or the consequences to the persons on the receiving end. Holloway has spent much of his career working in disadvantaged areas of Scotland and became a leader in the challenge to his church over the ordination of women and the acceptance of gay, lesbian, transgender and bisexual people. He has written many books describing his evolving ideas but in his "must read" autobiography, *Leaving Alexandria: a memoir of faith and doubt*,[144] Holloway describes, in a moving, highly personal account, his struggle with doubt from early adulthood, culminating in his resignation as a Bishop in 2000. For Holloway, those who preach certainty in religion about things we can really never know and must always see as mystery, harm the whole Christian enterprise by shaping God in their own non-negotiable images and the life of Jesus in a sole scenario of cosmic sacrifice that must be believed.

It is significant that the current Progressive Christianity movement has been fuelled for the most part from outside the institutional church hierarchy, often by lay people seeking answers. In groups in Australia, the majority of clergy involved are retired, not longer constrained by those intent on preserving the traditions, or pressured by the hierarchy not to rock the doctrinal boat too roughly. As one of this group's presenters, I hear a recurring cry from lay people wherever I present — "Why weren't we told?"[145] Etched on my memory are many distressed faces when people discover that doubts they have nursed for decades are valid and that many clergy have known this for years but have not been prepared to be whistle-blowers.

When confronted by this, clergy say that they did not want to disturb those in the pews who have no doubts, or that they have experienced pressure from powerful lay people within their congregations who reject new ideas. Unfortunately, the latter is a reality as many clergy and priests have been "outed" to church hierarchies for raising radical questions or challenging ecclesiastical rules within their congregations, with threats of demotion or censoring — many churches are *still* not hospitable places. Father Peter Kennedy (1938-) now leads his Catholic congregation, St. Mary's in Exile, in Brisbane Australia's Trades and Labour Council building, having been banned from officiating as a Catholic priest anywhere in Australia. Despite his overflowing, inclusive St. Mary's Church community of over one thousand people, with story after story of the abandoned and lonely finding hospitality and faith there, this meant nothing to the Roman Catholic hierarchy when Father Kennedy disobeyed correct procedures. His "sins" included allowing women to preach, blessing same-sex unions and changing the liturgy, most notably the baptismal formula, by using the non-gendered "Creator, Sustainer, Redeemer" instead of Father, Son and Holy Spirit. The hierarchy declared such baptisms already performed as invalid and banned him.

Progressive Christianity groups draw on contemporary research and writing, freeing Christianity from centring on many hard-to-believe dogmas that were not central to Jesus' message, asking instead how we should *live* in this world. [146] When Jesus was asked of the commandments (there were many more than ten) which was the most important, he listed a lifestyle rather than a doctrine — "Love God and love your neighbour as yourself" (Mark 12: 29-31). Over the centuries, however, the Christian church has become more like the Pharisees quibbling over whether or not hungry disciples should pick grain to eat on the Sabbath (Mark 2: 23-8) rather than how to feed the hungry. The no-nonsense words from Jesus were "The Sabbath [or substitute church here] was made for humankind and not humankind for the Sabbath" (v.27). To take this seriously, we need to step back a bit and see whether our churches and their doctrines-to-be-believed are demanding our obedience or enabling our freedom.

Progressive Christianity does not wish for a new creed or set of beliefs that everyone should espouse. Rather, it sees the initial task as deconstructing doctrines and dogmas that are crumbling around us because of their entrapment in language and concepts of the fourth century or medieval monasteries, with no recognition of the changes in the twenty-first century. People need to think for themselves by being provided with contemporary scholarship that can dialogue with contemporary worldviews. Progressive thinking has been around for centuries in different pockets and places. The difference today is that this movement is being named and the responsibility for its survival is in the hands of *laity* as well as clergy who will not be silenced into blind obedience and belief. With so many theologians of all persuasions now writing for the public market, access to new scholarship and thinking is now possible for all.

Progressive Christianity is also very careful not to create new prisons of "what-we-must-believe". Progressives themselves stand on a continuum of thought, some going much further than others in their rejection of traditional arguments, but there is a conscious effort to keep Progressive groups as safe places for people taking first tentative steps into critiquing the old and discovering new ways of thinking. The emphasis is about being on the way and having permission to doubt rather than signing on the dotted line for a new set of rules. Various Progressive groups have tried to produce statements of beliefs at different times but there is great hesitancy to codify this across the movement in any universal way. As the feminist movement discovered, when you allow people to trust their experience as a guide to life and think for themselves, you find a great diversity of conclusions.

For centuries, religions have made a first class job of packaging ultimate, unchallengeable claims in neatly interlocking doctrines which, like rows of dominoes, may collapse if one section fails. Not only must these doctrines be believed but those who doubt are made to feel there is something wrong with *them* if they raise questions. The best-kept secret of religious leaders and scholars today – that many of these doctrines are leaking like sieves – is at last becoming public knowledge, quite a change from when this book was first published. Doubt is being vindicated for what it is in most other disciplines, the honest, creative response to inconsistencies, outdated truth and oppressive authoritarianism. It is not that all tradition is wrong — that would be a travesty of everything that has shaped us in the past. Rather, this is a call to do what we do in every other discipline — think for ourselves and listen to our own experiences and the context in which we live.

We have been convinced over the centuries that certainty is the religious goal, the place of arrival. "Having faith" has equalled certainty and the more certain of everything we are, the greater the faith. A friend of mine was exploring all the new progressive possibilities of thinking and becoming very excited about it. When I talked to a mutual friend about her, however, who was still in the old traditions our friend was escaping, she said "Oh, she's lost her faith". More of us need to "lose our faith" if this is the case. Richard Holloway writes:

> [The] perils of being right points to one of the dangers of religion: our certainties — in a world where so little is certain — can make us haters and persecutors of the certainties of others, something that religion is all too prone to. But in contrast ... our doubts and loves can cause all sorts of lovely flowers to bloom, such as tolerance and compassion ... Faith has to be co-active with doubt or it is not faith but its opposite, certainty. More faith and less certainty would make the religions of the world more humble and compassionate, something that is devoutly to be wished. [147]

---

[137] Armstrong, *The Spiral Staircase,* 168

[138] The writers included Frederick William Temple, Headmaster of Rugby, Rowland Williams, Professor of Hebrew, Baden Powell, Oxford professor of Geometry, Henry Wilson, Professor of Anglo-Saxon and a parson, Charles Goodwin, a Cambridge layperson, Mark Pattison, Anglican divine and Benjamin Jowett, Plato expert and Master of Balliol College, Oxford.

[139] Benjamin Jowett, quoted in Geoffrey Faber, *Jowett: a portrait and background* (Cambridge, Mass: Harvard University Press, 1957), 245

[140] Randal Keynes, *Darwin, his Daughter, and Human Evolution* (New York: Riverhead Books, 2001), 145

[141] Keynes, *Darwin, his Daughter, and Human Evolution,* 145

[142] Albert Schweitzer, *Out of my Life and Thought* (New York: Mentor Books, 1933, 1936), 45

[143] *Living in Sin? A Bishop Rethinks Human Sexuality, Rescuing the Bible from Fundamentalism: A Bishop Rethinks the Meaning of Scripture, Born of a Woman: A Bishop Rethinks the Birth of Jesus, Resurrection: Myth or Reality? A Bishop's Search for the Origins of Christianity,*

[144] Richard Holloway, *Leaving Alexandria: a memoir of faith and doubt* (Melbourne: Text Publishing, 2012)

[145] A new book on Progressive Christianity is being published at the end of 2012. Rex A. E. Hunt & John W. H. Smith, editors and compilers, *We Weren't Told! A handbook on Progressive Christianity* (Salem, OR: Polebridge Press, 2012) For further information on Progressive Christianity, this is recommended.

[146] Useful Progressive Christianity websites are www.ProgressiveChristianity.org, www.westarinstitute.org, www.livingthequestions.com. www.johnshelbyspong.com, www.pcnbritain.org.uk, www.rexaehuntprogressive.com, pcnvictoria.blogspot.com, www.johndominiccrossan.com, www.valwebb.com.au

[147] Richard Holloway, quoted in *A World of Prayer,* Rosalind Bradley ed. (Maryknoll, New York: Orbis Books 2012), 77

Chapter 12.   The Interfaith Dialogue

I love you, my brother, whoever you are - whether you worship in your
church, kneel in your temple, or pray in your mosque. You and I are all
children of one faith, for the divers paths of religion are fingers of the
loving hand of one Supreme Being,
a hand extended to all, offering completeness of spirit to all,
eager to receive all.

Kahlil Gibran (1883-1931) [148]

One of the biggest questions to raise its head in the doubts department
is how the uniqueness of Jesus claimed by Christianity relates to other world
religions.   If doubts surface over doctrines about Jesus *within* our own
tradition, how do we deal with doubts about Jesus as the only way in light of
the wider world of religions?   In today's global village, our next door
neighbour may be Muslim, Mormon or Hindu. If we say that the unity that
binds us together in our diverse journeys is unconditional love and
compassion for each other, what about people of different religions? Fifty
years ago, this was not such a problem because distance and national
isolation allowed us to treat such people as "other". We can no longer do
that.   We are close neighbours and, as such, we are a community of
diversity.

How does our model of love, compassion and respect accommodate
this new situation? Can we really look at a devout Buddhist and declare that
there is no "truth" in her tradition? Can we watch a Muslim at prayer and
dismiss him as misguided? Each tradition has experiences of a Ground of
Being, producing mystics and martyrs of exemplary dedication and
conviction.   Have we the right to suggest, because of our particular
culturally bound dogmas, that all others are totally deluded? The Navajo
speaks of the journey as being "on the gleaming way". Have we the right to
look at that proud man and say his way is wrong? Has not this been the
curse of history, the root of war and hostility, of persecution and hatred?
These questions are difficult to ignore today because they may not come
from within our circle but be asked directly of us by our neighbours of a

different faith. Pluralism of religions is here to stay and responsible Christians have to address the issue.

As we have done in previous chapters, a look at church history throws interesting light on the question. The first Christians *also* lived in a pluralistic world. The Way of Jesus had emerged within Judaism but was also located in the cosmopolitan world of Greek and Roman thought, mystery religions and philosophy. From these different influences, Christianity "borrowed" imagery and thought forms that most helpfully expressed what they had encountered in Jesus. While the followers of Jesus in Jerusalem remained Jewish in tradition, Paul adapted to the Gentile world-view in order to preach good news to them. Later, the church fathers developed Christian creeds and doctrines with liberal borrowing of philosophical concepts from the "pagan" Greeks. Thus it is not possible to ask questions about who Jesus was without first locating Jesus both as a Jew *and* within a cosmopolitan Roman Empire heavily influenced by Greek thought.

After Emperor Constantine (272-337) accepted Christianity as a tolerated religion of the empire in the fourth century, those Christians previously persecuted for their faith became the persecutors of other religions and also other brands of Christianity with which they disagreed — "heresies". "Orthodox" Christianity would soon become *the* religion of the empire. Thus the centuries until the Reformation saw the unchallenged rise of the sovereignty of the Roman Church, together with the conviction of no salvation outside this church. This exclusivity would launch the Crusades against the infidel Muslims.

The Reformation also adopted a negative approach to other religions, continuing the belief that there was no salvation outside Christianity. Scripture became the reformers' only authority and selected scripture passages were used to reject other religions outright. Most notable was Martin Luther's treatises against the Jews, including *On the Jews and their Lies* which still causes consternation for Luther fans today. The advent of exploration and missionary activity by both Jesuits and pietistic Protestants and the influence of the Enlightenment however, forced a rethink of such an exclusive attitude. Frederick Schleiermacher, who tried to salvage Christian faith after the Enlightenment, was more open to other religions as containing truth, although he did see Christianity as the superior religion.

German protestant theologian Ernst Troeltsch continued this line of argument but changed his mind towards the end of his life. In his last essay, delivered posthumously in 1923, Troeltsch said that Christianity could not be judged as better than other religions because it is imperialistic to compare other religions in terms of *our* cultural understandings rather than theirs. For him, any religion was relative to its culture. We can talk together and be tolerant of the other; we can commit to our truth, live and die for it, yet realize that it is not universal truth but rather truth *for us*. This was a radical move at a time when colonialism and missionary activities were alive and well around the world. Troeltsch opened the door for many at the turn of the nineteenth century to investigate other religions with confidence and see value in them for what they offered in their particular culture.

While Troeltsch saw all religions as relative, partial, and limited, historian Arnold Toynbee (1889-1975) argued that all religions are essentially the same — different paths leading to a common essence, God. While there may be a common core, their expressions in various cultural and political settings are different. To him, the exclusive claims to God which Christians made were a sin. Toynbee was ahead of his time and was rejected by both the historians and the theologians, but his thoughts are echoed in many areas of interreligious dialogue today.

Psychologist Carl Jung also saw a common core in all religions but he saw their commonality arising from the human psyche. In the collective unconscious, there are archetypes common to all, but decoded differently in religious symbols and myths. The God-image is part of this collective unconscious that confronts *our* unconscious and helps us realize our own selves. In this scenario, Jesus was the most highly differentiated symbol of a self, although Jung saw the Buddha also in this class and wanted to dialogue with Buddhism for a better understanding of the unconscious.

Christian responses to other religions in the twentieth and twenty-first centuries sit at different places on a continuum. The key issue is Christology - who Jesus was and what was his mission. Responses can be divided into three rough categories — exclusivists, inclusivists and pluralists. Exclusivists believe that salvation and eternal life come only through the sacrificial death of Jesus Christ, Son of God and part of the Trinity, which occurred once for all. Salvation is gained by belief in the efficacy of this event, thus there can be no salvation in any other religion as

Christ does not save through any other religion. Dialogue with other faiths is therefore only in order to convert them. Inclusivists see some truth in many religions as different responses to the Divine. God can be revealed, through nature and history, in other religions, but salvation is found only through the Christian story. One could ask, however, why God would reveal the divine self in another religion without also offering salvation in that tradition?

The Catholic Church has been more open to other religions than many other Christian denominations. Before Vatican II (1962-65), Catholic theologians struggled to hold together belief in God's universal desire to save and the idea that there is no salvation outside their church. When the New World was being colonized, the idea that some people were "baptized by desire" was introduced — indigenous people who lived good moral lives even though they had never heard of Christ or the church were baptized by their desire to be good. Vatican II moved further by declaring that anyone who had not heard of Jesus but followed their conscience was moved by grace and could partake in eternal life through the church. Theologian Karl Rahner (1904-84) introduced the term "anonymous Christian". Buddhists and Hindus living a virtuous life were actually saved by Christ through the church, even if they did not know it. Of course, if they were then exposed to Christianity, their salvation depended on whether they then accepted the church's teaching and were officially baptized into Christianity.

The third attitude to other religions is pluralism which sees all religions as different expressions of the one Ultimate Reality. We cannot rank religions as good or bad, better or worse, but as valid but different expressions of the same search for meaning. Theologian John Hick said:

> As human productions, these spiritual homes are all inevitably limited and imperfect, each having its own distinctive strengths and weaknesses, advantages and disadvantages. And in the new ecumenical age which we are now entering, the religious traditions will increasingly interact with one another and affect one another's further development, enabling each to learn, we may hope, from the others' insights and benefit from the others' virtues. [149]

This does not mean that all religions are the same — they are different in what they see as the "human condition", that awareness that something is wrong with the world. Religion seeks to answer the questions stemming from this — what do we want to be and how do we get there? As a general rule, Middle Eastern religions (Judaism, Christianity and Islam) see the human problem as "sin" and the solution as forgiveness and restoration of relations with God. Religions arising in India (Hinduism and Buddhism) see the human condition as ignorance of our true nature and thus we grasp at external, fleeting things. The solution is to let go and discover our true self within. For Hindus, their individual self, *atman*, is actually the Universal Self, *Brahman*. For Buddhists, in realizing *no-self*, they become "buddhas" or enlightened ones. In Chinese religions (Confucianism and Daoism), the human condition is disharmony with self, society and the universe and the solution is restoration of the natural balance — by education and a structured society in Confucianism; and through the *Dao* (*Tao*) in Daoism, that mysterious way of nature and power that maintains harmony. For indigenous religious traditions, separation and alienation from land/earth/nature results in "lostness" and the solution is to re-bind themselves to the Sacred present in/with/around them through story and ritual. From this we can see that trying to convince "heathens" of their "sins" so they can leave this earth for a better heaven will be entirely foreign to them if *their* concern is being separated from the earth and their solution is to bind themselves more closely to it as mother.

What then do we do with the Christian claim of a unique divine incarnation in Jesus Christ? As I have already mentioned, contemporary scholars have looked again at Jesus and sought to remove the layers of theological accretions over the centuries that changed the life and teachings of the Jewish man Jesus into the second person of the divine Trinity. The doctrine of the Trinity (God as Father, Son and Spirit) was not spelled out as such in the Bible but became established by the fourth century when the bishops of the church in their church councils were still arguing as to whether Jesus was God, or *like* God. This tells us that the divinity of Jesus was not the earliest understanding within Christianity. The Jewish idea of "messiah" was not a supernatural God-man but a flesh-and-blood man drawn from among them and anointed by God for a special task. "Son of God" was not originally used as a biological term depicting divinity, but a title for many in Israel with a special relationship with God — kings (Psalm 2: 7) righteous individuals (Wisdom of Solomon 2:18), angels (Job 38: 7) and even all Israel (Hosea 11:1). [150] It was also used for the Roman Caesar in Jesus' time as one considered divine, as was the title "saviour" as "saviour of the people". According to biblical scholar John Dominic Crossan, these titles for the Roman Caesars were used for Jesus by his followers as a challenge, to proclaim Jesus' vision of an alternate empire or kingdom of God, one of non-violence, compassion, justice and peace. Crossan says:

> It is the radicality of God's justice and not the normalcy of civilization's injustice that ... I find incarnate in Jesus of Nazareth ... the good news, as ... seen from Jesus and Paul, is that the violent normalcy of human civilization is *not* the inevitable destiny of human nature. [151]

While this is not the place for a full discussion of Jesus scholarship, it is enough to say to doubters that Christianity no longer offers only one interpretation of Jesus' person and mission.

John Hick sees "incarnation" as the incarnation of God's *love* in Jesus. God was *in* the man Jesus in the sense that Jesus' *love* was fully God's love at work in him. Since God's love or Spirit is universal, God is truly encountered in Jesus but not necessarily *only* in Jesus. Thus Jesus can be the centre and norm for Christians as an expression of God's Spirit within without having to be the only centre of God's incarnational presence in religion.

> People can be fully committed to the God they discover through Jesus, a man so distinctly open to the Divine Spirit in his day, without having to make absolute claims, especially when [Jesus'] immediate followers did not make such claims. [152]

For many today, absolute claims are unethical and ideas of Jesus as the "only" have brought disaster for the world through wars and hatred between religions. By centring on Ultimate Reality/Source/the Real/God/ Sacred as common ground for religions, each can respect the particularities of the other as expressions of Ultimate activity without demanding that all adopt the cultural/historical particularity of God's activity in Jesus. Of course, there will be those who absolutely condemn these ideas but, for the doubter, it is affirming to know that reputable scholars comfortably sit at all points along a range of opinion.

If we imagine God as the Spirit of the universe within us and within everything else in an interconnected organic whole, that means that this Spirit is not limited to our own humanly created and culturally limited doctrines and experience of history but has been writing a broader and more diverse history in many worlds, languages and with many pens for more epochs than our culture even knows about. If we do not believe this, we have not been reading our Bible. The psalmist says:

> Where can I go from your spirit
> Or where can I flee from your presence?
> If I ascend to heaven, you are there:
> If I make my bed in Sheol, you are there.
> If I take the wings of the morning
> and settle at the farthest limits of the sea,
> even there your hand shall lead me
> and your right hand shall hold me fast. (Ps. 139: 7-10)

Earlier I said that what can draw us all together as human beings on a religious quest is love and compassion. Interestingly, the one thing that all the founders of faith traditions across the world stumbled on as the key to life, peace and well-being was *compassion* or, in the words of the Golden Rule, "do to others as you would like them to do to you". Christians have long assumed that the Golden Rule began with Jesus but this simply shows our ignorance of others. Ancient wisdom from Sumatra says, "Let all your undertakings be pleasing to you, as well as others. If that is not possible, at least do not harm anyone".[153] Zoroastrian sacred texts say, "*That* nature alone is good, which refrains from doing unto another whatsoever is not good for itself". From the Hindu Vedic texts, "This is the sum of duty. Do nothing unto others which would cause you pain if done to you". Confucius said, "What one does not wish for oneself, one ought not to do to anyone else; what one recognizes as desirable for oneself, one ought to be willing to grant to others". From Plato, "May I do to others as I would that they should do to me". The Jewish Talmud says, "What is hateful to you, do not to your fellow human being: this is the whole Torah: while the rest is the commentary thereof ...". From the Buddha, "Hurt not others in ways that you yourself would find hurtful". When we hear these – and there are more — the words ascribed to Jesus in Matthew, "So in everything, do to others what you would have them do to you" seem strangely less unique. And Jesus acknowledged this, adding that this "sums up all of the Law and of the prophets".[154] Human beings have thus long recognized the centrality of compassion and codified it within their various religious traditions.

In 2007, religion scholar Karen Armstrong won a monetary TED award (Technology, Entertainment, Design) to pursue her dream of a global community where people live together in mutual respect. While religions should be in the *forefront* of this, many focus instead on secondary issues of sexual practices and obtuse doctrinal definitions. Global conflicts that are basically fuelled by greed, power, hatred, envy and ambition have been labelled as *holy* wars defending a God perfectly capable of self-defence and spawning terrorist attacks or hate crimes against those whose beliefs or lifestyles are deemed wrong. Armstrong has initiated a *Charter for Compassion* written by leaders across religions, calling for a restoration of the Golden Rule to the *heart* of religions to counter voices of extremism, intolerance and hatred.[155] The Charter says:

> Compassion impels us to work tirelessly to alleviate the suffering of our fellow creatures, to dethrone ourselves from the centre of our world and put another there, and to honour the inviolable sanctity of every single human being, treating everybody, without exception, with absolute justice, equity and respect ... To act or speak violently out of spite, chauvinism or self-interest, to impoverish, exploit or deny basic rights to anybody, and to incite hatred by denigrating others — even our enemies — is a denial of our common humanity. We acknowledge that we have failed to live compassionately and that some have even increased the sum of human misery in the name of religion. [156]

When compassion is spelled out in these terms, no one has to point out how we have failed miserably as individuals, nations and global citizens. Yet the goals sound impractical, impossible and perhaps inadvisable to many who also interpret Jesus' "turn the other cheek" nonsense as metaphorical exaggeration. Yet when we think of examples of goodness and nobility in our world, we name the Mother Teresa's, the Florence Nightingale's, the Gandhi's and the Martin Luther King's rather than CEO's, sports heroes and politicians — people who took their compassion for the oppressed and outcast seriously enough to fight for their dignity against all odds.

The actual *Charter of Compassion* reads: We therefore call upon all men and women

- to restore compassion to the centre of morality and religion

- to return to the ancient principle that any interpretation of scripture that breeds violence, hatred or disdain, is illegitimate

- to ensure that youth are given accurate and respectful information about other traditions, religions and cultures

- to encourage a positive appreciation of cultural and religious diversity

- to cultivate an informed empathy with the suffering of all human beings - even those regarded as enemies [157]

In expanding this discussion and its possibilities, the Charter says:

> We urgently need to make compassion a clear, luminous and dynamic force in our polarized world. Rooted in a principled determination to transcend selfishness, compassion can break down political, dogmatic, ideological and religious boundaries. Born of our deep interdependence, compassion is essential to human relationships and to a fulfilled humanity. It is the path to enlightenment, and indispensable to the creation of a just economy and a peaceful global community. [158]

As I write, over 76,000 have added their names to this Charter, translated into thirty languages. But adding a name is not all. On the Charter website, people are asked to post their specific commitment to an act of compassion in their area.

Talking together is not only about finding commonalities but also learning from our differences. Contradictions often become merely contrasts, different ways of seeing something that can stand side by side, not as either/or. Philosopher William James (1842-1910) said, in talking about "truth", "You can take a chess-board as black squares on a white ground, or as white squares on a black ground, and neither conception is a false one". [159] What brings us together is the *desire* to be in dialogue. Openness in dialogue allows each to be who we are, to have a position which is important to us, but to trust that we need not cling to that for all time but be in a *process* of learning and growing, wherever that may take us. This approach is very comforting for the doubter. We can look at the question of other religions as another nudge to be addressed and experience new richness from each other without losing the uniqueness *for us* of the claims we each make.

An open interest in, and respect for, other religions has been a rude shock to some Western Christians who feel their brand of religion is far superior to all others and refuse to believe that God may also be at work in other religions. What is even more shocking for such people is the realization that seekers from the East have *tried* our Western product and rejected it in favour of their original traditions. Satomi Myodo (1896-1978), a Japanese woman searching for meaning with a drivenness that believed there *was* a way to discover, wrote of her experience:

> I ran to religious meetings here and there, fishing among the old, established religions and the new religions, taking them as equal. Most of them though, were rehashed morality or warmed-over mysteries, or again, a drop of this and a dash of that, offered up in a cocktail. In the end all they said was that their own sect was right..... When I realized that, unlike other faiths in which one prays for benefits or miracles, in Buddhism one neither hates hell nor hopes for heaven, but rather lives courageously and eternally in the world of karma, I felt keenly that only here was true liberation to be found. [160]

From the point of view of an educated Buddhist, it is Western intolerance and imperialism for Christianity to declare, as we have in the past, that our thoughts are the only valid thoughts, without even listening to teachings others holds dear. Contemplative monk Thomas Merton went to Asia in the sixties to learn what the ancient monastic traditions of the East could teach him of benefit to his monastic Christian life. He said:

> I think we have now reached a stage (long overdue) of religious maturity at which it may be possible for someone to remain perfectly faithful to a Christian and Western monastic commitment, and yet to learn in depth from, say, a Buddhist discipline and experience. [161]

The distinction of "belief" and "faith" discussed in the first chapter helps interfaith dialogue. Belief is the system of doctrines while faith is a relationship with, or awareness of, something bigger than oneself, whether it be interconnectedness in a living organic universe or something we might call God. Faith, therefore, is not the exclusive property of any one religion. The hope for communion with, and compassion for, those of other religious traditions is that we look away from dogma and grasp what we have in common - faith, that internal response of our hearts to the tugging of love from whatever it is that is greater or broader or deeper than us. Just as this book challenges us to allow people within their church community the right to experience God in their own way in an hospitable environment, the challenge is also to do this on a global level. The first step is to affirm the validity of all to own their faith experiences in the journey of being human:

> ......a man's [or woman's] effort to understand why he is in the world and what he ought to be doing about it has attracted many of the finest minds of which we have record. Over the centuries man and women, in many languages and in terms often - though not invariably - borrowed from the prevailing religion or philosophy, have felt impelled to ask themselves crucial questions about their identity and destiny, and about the design and maintenance of the miraculously beautiful universe in which we so inexplicably find ourselves....The questions that preclude such a search have not ceased to trouble mankind, despite the fact that no sure answers have been forthcoming and in all probability never will be. Nonetheless some who have travelled this road have fared further and over their shoulders, as it were, have thrown back "hints and guesses". Although their voices have been carried down the wind, and, in many cases, were often couched in allusive and allegorical language, they may still embody guidance about the nature of the quest and the pitfalls on the road. [162]

Unity is not to assume that we should find some way to synthesize all religions into one. It is not to deny or gloss over differences. It is not to claim that every aspect of every religion is equally valid. The invitation here is rather the permission to examine the question of other religions with honesty, to adopt an open position towards those of other persuasions that allows us to talk, to listen, to share, to love, always with the possibility that each of us will learn from the other. This is hospitality - love in action.

My case rests. The invitation to doubt has been extended, to cherish and nurture doubts as sacred gifts that lead into richness and freedom. Freedom is to doubt so boldly that all issues of belief and faith can gain a hearing. What is the promise? Not constant sunshine, instant success, unlimited wealth, immortal health, or a personal genie. Rather, it is the hope that, if we open the windows of our lives and allow fresh winds to blow through - and sometimes cyclones, tornadoes and thunderstorms - we will also recognize a caress that lightly touches our face, or the inner joy of interconnectedness with the universe and with something many call God.

---

[148] Kahlil Gibran, *The Wisdom of Gibran,* Joseph Sheban, ed. (New York: Philosophical Library, 1966), 17

[149] Hick, *God Has Many Names,* 21

[150] Paul J. Achtemeier, gen ed., *Harper's Bible Dictionary* (New York: HarperSanFrancisco, 1985), 979

[151] John Dominic Crossan, *God and Empire: Jesus against Rome, then and now* (New York: HarperSanFrancisco, 2007) 224, 238, 241 - 2.

[152] Webb, *Like Catching Water in a Net,* 208

[153] The following quotations of the Golden Rule can be found in Anand Krishna, *One Earth, One Sky, One Humankind: celebration of unity in diversity* (Jakata: PT Gramedia Pustaka Utama Publishing) 113, 19, 57, 99, 117, 35, 107

[154] Matthew 7:12

[155] Armstrong, *Twelve Steps,* 6

[156] Armstrong, *Twelve Steps,* 7

[157] Armstrong, *Twelve Steps,* 7

[158] Armstrong, *Twelve Steps,* 8

[159] William James, quoted in Bradley, Daniels & Jones, compilers, *The International Dictionary of Thoughts,* 736

[160] Satomi Myodo, *Passionate Journey: the spiritual autobiography of Satomi Myodo,* Sallie B. King trans. & annotator (Boston: Publications Inc., 1987), 70,84,91

[161] Amiya Chakravarty, consulting ed., *The Asian Journal of Thomas Merton* (New York: New Directions Publishing Corp., 1968), xxiii

[162] Cecil, Rieu, Wade, compilers, *The King's Son,* xv-xvi

Lightning Source UK Ltd.
Milton Keynes UK
UKOW07f0136030315

247190UK00001B/30/P